60, SEX & TANGO
Confessions of a Beatnik Boomer
by Joan Moran

To my mother, Estelle
Stella by Starlight
1911–2009

CONTENTS
FOREWORD
ACKNOWLEDGMENTS
INTRODUCTION
TURN ON, TUNE IN, DROP OUT

PART ONE: 60 — 1
CHAPTER 1
YIN AND YANG — 3
Future Perfect — 5
Bringing In The Sheaves — 7
One Step Forward, Two Steps Back — 11
On The Road — 12

CHAPTER 2
GET RID OF THE SCRIPT — 15
Tango X Two — 16
Do You Believe In Magic? — 19
Don't Drink The Kool-Aid — 20
Where Angels Fear To Tread — 22

CHAPTER 3
YOUR CHILDREN ARE GROWN, GET OVER IT — 25
Changing The Urban Floor Plan — 27
Reading Tea Leaves Or How Ancestor Worship Fell Into Disrepute — 28
The Wandering Jewess — 31
On The Way To The Holy Grail — 36
Thank You, Dr. Freud — 37
I'm Dancing As Fast As I Can — 38
All In The Family — 40
When A Parent Becomes The Child — 41
The Wedding Crasher — 44

CHAPTER 4
BACK TO THERAPY: MI VIDA LOCA 46
So Jung 49
Stop the World, I Want to Get Off 50
Wedding Bell Blues 53
Ride a Painted Pony 55
Epilogue: Watch Out for That Curveball 57

CHAPTER 5
DON'T CALL ME GRANDMA! 58
Call Me Gran 59
Who's On First? 61
Who's On Second? 62
Like Mother, Like Daughter 68
Under One Roof 69

PART TWO: SEX 71
CHAPTER 6
MEN AND OTHER SOCIOPATHS I HAVE KNOWN 72
A Hard Act To Follow 75
Confessions Of An Internet Dater 82
Bless Me, Father, For I Have Sinned 91
Let's Make A Deal 93
Matchmaker, Matchmaker, Make Me A Match 97
Movin' On Down The Highway 98
Searching for Intelligent Signs 99

CHAPTER 7
IS HE CHEAP, OR IS HIS HAND STUCK IN HIS POCKET? 102
A Few Good Men 103
The Art Of Cheaposity 106
A Few Bad Men 108
I Am Woman: Hear Me Roar 114
Made In America 116

CHAPTER 8
THONGS I HAVE WORN 118
I've Got You Under My Skin 119
I'm Too Sexy For My Uniform 120
Searching For Jack Kerouac 121
Like A Virgin 122
Berkeley In The 60s 123
It's Vegas, Baby, Vegas 124
Send In The Clowns, There Ought To Be Clowns 127
The Art Of The Deal 128
Sex With Benefits: No Expiration Date Needed 134
It's A Vicious Rumor 137
The Tao Of Sex Toys 138

CHAPTER 9
WHEN YOUR BEST FRIEND IS NOT YOUR LOVER 142
Get A Wrecking Crew And Clean Up This Mess 144
Get Out Of Your Cave And Find Some Light, Dude 145
It Hurts So Good 148
Bloody English 149
A Bird In The Hand 150
Oldies But Not Goodies 153
The Male Mystique 156
Where, O Where Have All The Flowers Gone? 158

PART THREE: TANGO 161
CHAPTER 10
HE DID IT HIS WAY 162

CHAPTER 11
BEING ALONE: IT HURTS SO GOOD 164
Hell's Kitchen 165
Separate Tables 166
The Pleasure Chest 168
The Way We Were 169

Oh, Brother, Where Art Thou? 174
Let's Hang On To What We've Got 175
Curiosity Did Not Kill The Cat 178
Forget Your Troubles, Come On, Get Happy 180
The Best Revenge 184
Here Comes Da Judge 185
Shedding My Skin: Snakes Do It 185

CHAPTER 12
GOTTA GET OUT OF DODGE 187
The Greatest Show On Earth 187
Timbuktu And Other Places To Hide 189
Time In A Bottle 190
Don't Put Your Label On Me 192
The Dreaded "R" Word 193
With Retirement, You Get Egg Roll 196
Living La Vida Loca 201

CHAPTER 13
CONVERSATIONS WITH MYSELF 203
Ashes To Ashes 204
Becoming On Becoming 209
My Mother, Myself 211
Thinking Outside The Mat 213
I Feel Pretty, Oh So Pretty, I Feel Pretty And Witty And Wise 216
I'm Beginning To Feel My Ears: Plastic Surgery And Other Cures 219
Don't Believe Everything You Think 220
I Feel The Earth Move 225

CHAPTER 14
CALM TO THE CORE 227
It Takes Two 229
But It Really Takes One 232
Forgiving Is A Bitch 237
I'm Over It 241

EPILOGUE 244
NOTES 247

FOREWORD

I met Joan eight years ago when I was a student in a yoga class she taught on the beach in Venice, California. Since then, I have followed her to several yoga studios, until she and I decided that she would conduct a small private class in my living room, a situation I am quite pleased with since it only requires me to stumble out of bed and walk down the hall.

Over the years, Joan evolved from being my beautiful, preternaturally youthful yoga mentor to a dear and trusted friend. Together, we have braved several tumultuous relationships (hers), cancer (mine), and issues with children and loss.

Joan is many things in addition to being a yoga instructor. She is a tango dancer and teacher, a drug and alcohol counselor, and a writer. Everything she sets out to do she attacks with passion, determination, style, flair, and heaps of humor. She has earned every penny to her name because of her highly disciplined nature and emotional dedication to her work. Her only flaw might be that Joan always asks for less than what she gives.

About a year and a half ago, Joan told me she wanted to write this book. She thought my advice would be helpful since I am a social psychologist and would have my own unique assessment of her material. She allowed me to read and comment on various drafts as it took shape and, finally, in its finished form.

I found *60, Sex & Tango* more than a book about the aging process and coming to terms with being sixty. The themes in Joan's book are deeper and embrace a less-obvious but much-needed spiritual perspective as it relates to an entire generation that is growing older. In addition, Joan discourses about the study of yoga and meditation, sprinkled with key elements of Buddhism and Jungian psychology, bringing significant substance to her book.

60, Sex & Tango also relates to the pull our past has on us and how that past shapes and informs our daily lives. Yes, Joan's book is about being a baby boomer; but it is as a single mother, a daughter, a grandmother, a mother-in-law, a breadwinner and a lover that makes 60, Sex, & Tango come alive with emotional revelations that any reader can identify with, no matter the age. Her sections on falling in love with dysfunctional men, as well as her adventures in online dating and tango dancing, are truly humorous and engaging, to say nothing of being dead-on accurate.

When all is said and done, Joan writes simply and eloquently about waking up each morning and going through the day with dignity, grace, and humor—no matter the age, no matter the difficulties, no matter the struggles, no matter the disappointments. For Joan, living large in her sixth decade is living life at full-throttle energy combined with an earthy élan, a romantic sensibility, and self-effacing humor. She is always ready to embrace the unexpected and roll with the punches.

Joan knows what she's talking about, and this book has something to say no matter how old or how young. Enjoy.

Tina Moss
Social Psychologist, Los Angeles

ACKNOWLEDGMENTS

I wish to acknowledge the following people whose guidance and contributions to this book have been invaluable. It is no accident that those who have guided me on my journey into my sixties are inspirational and divine beings.

To my mother, for her unending belief in who I am
To my father, for his humor and love of history
To my sons, Jonathan and Aaron, for their love and primary material
To my grandsons—Jordan, Luc, Jude, and Greyson—for their joy
To my loving daughters-in-law, Carli and Alyse, for their love and support
To my wonderful therapist, Mike, who lead me on the conscious journey
To my primary eyes and ears, Tina Moss, the vortex
To Faye Swetzy and her assistant, D. J. Herta, for their belief
To Wendy Kush, for being my writing inspiration
To Kathy, for being the mistress of peace and calm
To Corinne, for beginning this journey with me
To my constant and loving friend, John Steiner, for being there every day
To Annie, for the party that is always going on and for a place to write
To Elisa, for support, love, and employment
To my ex-husband, for being the master of understatement
To my master teachers, Max Strom, Steve Ross, and Mark Stephens
To all my devoted yogis and yoginis at UCLA
To Camille and Janine, for being loving women of substance
To David, for his love and Zen

My writing journey has been a learning experience and a joy, but without the input and devotion of the people mentioned above, I would not have had as much fun.

Joan Moran

INTRODUCTION
TURN ON, TUNE IN, DROP OUT

On the night of November 10, I slipped into my queen-size bed, alone. I was sixty-three years old. I woke up the next morning on the eleventh of November, and as life would have it, I was sixty-four years old. I literally could not get out of bed. The accidental Jewess had quite suddenly stopped her wandering.

The lining of my throat felt like a burning cigarette as my postnasal drip kicked into action. The signs of illness were familiar. Either I was in the midst of neurosis or a sinus infection. But what gripped me hardly mattered.

I tried to push back the covers and roll out of bed, but I couldn't. My heart wasn't into it. It was Veterans Day, my birthday, and there were no classes at UCLA. Still, I had to teach a few private yoga classes. I tried again to find the strength to get up. I reached deep into the inner recesses of my redundant mind to find motivation. Was I having a panic attack or wallowing in self-pity? I pulled the covers back over my head and waited for a sign.

Entering my midsixties does not make me an expert in living. I'm not the person to give lessons in aging gracefully. I'm challenged, I'm insecure, I'm lonely, I'm in denial. I'm exploring and sifting through the remnants of life, lost family members, lost loves, lost friends, and lost dreams. I'm a woman who stayed on life's track by unconsciously tap-dancing my way through the good, the bad, and the ugly. Why was I feeling that hope and joy were the evil twin faces of illusion?

I needed a playbook to master my sixties. I wanted a guidebook, a cheat sheet, a course of study; otherwise, I would be forever walking sideways like a crab and asking the same question over and over again, why me? Why am I on the back nine? Because I'm not blasted ready yet!

I still feel like I'm nineteen. I still feel like I can break the glass ceiling. I still feel I may fall in love again. I still feel I could make love to two men in the same day, at different times, of course. I still love an occasional booty call. I know it's not cool to be middle-aged and retired, looking like an aging hippy, sprouting a skinny gray ponytail. How attractive is that engorged waistline in a swimsuit? And I'm not forgetting women in their sixties who think it's possible to still look hip wearing miniskirts or baby doll dresses with empire waists, too-tight jeans, and sleeveless tops that accentuate the ubiquitous sagging arms of women trying to turn back time. But fishnet stockings are still okay in my fashion book.

Did boomers think we would even get to the age of sixty? And even if we gave it a thought, did we somehow believe it would be a continuation of being fifty? The trendy mantra that the sixty is the new fifty is delusional because boomers believed that our world-weary intellect, over-the- top charm, and scintillating personalities would always give us an advantage over other generations.

But sixty is here and now, and what are we really going to do with the rest of our lives? How are we going to fill our free time and still look attractive enough to go on Match.com?

As boomers wind down the most productive years on the way to retirement, I am still working, still a single woman still looking for love in all the wrong places, and still living life in fits and starts. I worry that I am not close to gaining self-knowledge or even reaching the elusive state of personal transformation. Changes in attitudes and feelings take me by surprise. I am confused and restless, and I don't understand why or how being in my sixties feels so undefined.

I'm actually a fake boomer. I missed the cutoff by three years. Born in 1943, I am considered a World War II babe. There are 76 million boomers born between 1946 and 1964, and they make up 26 percent of the present population. I lumped myself into the boomer group because I identify with the zeitgeist. What's three years' difference anyway? Who's counting? Who cares? World War II was my parents' generation; and that meant identifying with the Depression, frugality, green stamps, and hamburger casseroles. My ex-husband has six years on the boomer brigade, and he thought he was as privileged and entitled as the other 76 million.

As a preboomer, I don't know how hip I was or how much I engendered the mantra of free love, but my spirit was full of activism, both politically and socially. And I was very proud that as a girl of twenty, I was present when the Beatles landed on the rooftop of the Sahara Hotel in Las Vegas, Nevada, in the summer of 1964.

London was our biggest influence. It was the birthplace of Carnaby Street, the mod look, Nehru jackets, the Beatles, and the Rolling Stones. America spawned Miles Davis, John Coltrane, Janis Joplin, Paul Simon and Art Garfunkel, Bob Dylan, Joan Baez, Joni Mitchell, Carole King, Jimi Hendrix, and so many genius musicians that the boomer generation took on a rarefied status that has never been replicated, thereby bankrupting future generations with the physical and mental realities of an aging population. We were identified with the radical protests of the 1970s; and we stand tall as the witnesses of the unrelenting moral morass of Vietnam, the tragedy of Kent State, and the mock trial of the Chicago Seven.

The boomers have been America's default setting for almost fifty years. And to our credit, we kept our identity alive by morphing into hippies and yuppies and buppies and kept on reinventing ourselves every decade to remind subsequent generations that we rock on with our ability to sustain our mythology.

But what did the boomers leave on the table? What was our contribution in the last fifty years besides enduring musicianship, a canon of great films that reflected our country's dark underbelly, retro clothes by designers no longer alive, a lot of drug use ending in not-so-anonymous deaths, and free love that didn't quite work out when everyone put their keys into a bowl?

As the boomers left the counterculture for the 1980s' "greed is good" mantra, we began to amass large quantities of goods and use gargantuan amounts of services. We fat cats hid our wealth behind bloated homes with big gates and manicured lawns. What boomer with too much money and an inflated ego wouldn't buy a gas-guzzling SUV, cultivate garish symbols of wealth, like stashes of bling, take ridiculously expensive trips to Kenya for safaris, or insist on giving riding lessons to spoiled little daughters who would never see a horse after puberty?

Frankly, boomers have been getting older for quite a while. Finally reaching sixty didn't make us more grown-up or smarter. Boomers hyped the praises of living a mature life more out of social unease and economic fear than our need to stay hip.

More to the point, when were we boomers ever going to ask ourselves if what motivated us on the way up would be enough to motivate us on the way out? I mean out as in "out of this life" when sickness and death are inevitable outcomes, and we can't buy our way out of dying. Death doesn't accept credit cards.

Now in our sixties, as our vulnerabilities strip away our hypocrisies, are we boomers ever going to discover the bliss of self-reflection? Is it even possible that we possess the insight to process our former self-absorbing and oftentimes-narcissistic behavior, laissez-faire child-raising paradigms, and self-destructive tendencies? No doubt we are an intelligent and well-educated group of men and women. We are competent and energetic. But we are also a glib group that often gives lip service to compassion and generosity. If being conscious isn't our strong suit, if empathy isn't a heartbeat away, what do we have left to work with?

There are so many significant changes taking place that boomers are in a constant state of flux. The "R" word (retirement) is becoming irrelevant; new interests are developing. The dynamics of our relationships are changing with husbands and wives, parents, and adult children; and social dating is on the agenda to satisfy the ego's need to be loved. Just when we thought we had mastered our self-esteem issues, we lose a job or a mate or a parent. And the piece de resistance is that we're definitely going to live longer because modern medicine can make that happen.

So, maybe, just possibly, there is time left for transformation, to reshape the course of our lives. The bad news is that we are witnessing profound economic and environmental challenges; the good news is that we still have our human faces on and our entrepreneurial skills intact.

My hope is that our collective unconscious will be able to sustain a new world order in which green is king and where truth, kindness, and fairness are the orders of the day. This new stage of adulthood and maturity might involve giving back to our communities through outreach, tutoring the young and disadvantaged, and serving abroad for educational and humanitarian efforts. Let our mantra be "Give back to the earth, solve problems and find solutions for crucial domestic and world issues, develop green industries, and volunteer to help those who are less fortunate."

After all is said and done, boomers carry the burden of the expectation of that illusive America dream, which we ourselves created.

So much for mythology.

I peeled the covers off my face the morning I turned sixty-four and found I was in a no-man's decade with memories of Berkeley in the sixties, the day Kennedy was shot, a long-ago divorce, a nest that had been empty for many years, three grandsons, a list of fairly decent lovers, the love of my life deceased, my mother nearing the end of her life, and the possibility that I will never fall in love again.

With trepidation and feeling of some hope, I got out of bed and embraced my sixties. It was about time!

This is my story about *60, Sex & Tango*. You have your own.

PART 1
60

Text message from my daughter-in-law Carli
We r @ The Make A Wish dinner,
ran into your best friend, Caroline...
she thinks u look the same as u did
30 years ago...so screw 64

CHAPTER 1
YIN AND YANG

I hate text messaging. It is not that I don't have a phone plan to include texting, it's not about the fifteen cents' charge on every text message (my sons say that I am the cheapest person they know), it's not about the typing because I type ninety words a minute, and it's not about the incredible frustration of not being able to fit your fingers on the keypad—unless you have long nails, and I don't have those.

No offense to the Israeli techies who invented texting, but the messaging system is off-putting. I prefer to hear a warm voice, like when a man asks you out for dinner or says you are really pretty, or even an angry voice, like when my adult children reprimand me for crossing boundaries because I was the one who finally got the pacifier out of my grandson's mouth. Call me old-fashioned because I think a phone call is more intimate, and texting has avoidance written all over it. Evidently, the state of California feels the same way I do because it banned texting while driving. Of course, that law was created in the vain hope of reducing traffic accidents in Los Angeles. No way. You can't get there from here.

I love the Israelis for working so hard to come up with new technologies, but text messaging was probably dreamed up by some guys attending Friday night Shabbat services when mental telepathy did not work. I've even lost dates over not texting back. Of course, they were not in my age-group.

The above text message from my daughter-in-law Carli is one

I will cherish forever because it spawned the idea to write a book about aging. The idea seemed simple enough. I'm a single woman in my sixties. I've lived a relatively long, healthy, productive, and loving life. A few of my friends tell me the reason that I am able to express myself so completely is because I am single and unattached. I can explore the nooks and crannies of living boldly since I don't have a man that gets in the way of my free expression. More germane to the aging process is my commitment to yoga as a practice of mind-body connection. So it appears that I am a full-on doer and a liver without boundaries. Energy, passion, and spiritual connection are the major themes on my journey.

I attribute the joy of living and committed passion of my life to my loving parents who raised me in a small town just north of San Francisco. It was the 1950s and early 1960s, and my childhood was happy and idyllic. I cannot say my upbringing paralleled the Leave It to Beaver universe, but there was love and support every step of the way. I was the quintessential "good girl" who followed the rules of my family and church. And I expected a happy life in return. Struggle and loss happened to people less fortunate, to those who did not possess the opportunities given to me by my parents.

My real life began to take shape in the upper echelons of higher education, at UCLA and Berkeley, where the world began to configure an alternative paradigm for living and loving. My mind opened to new ideas and new philosophies, and as a result, the Catholic Church's death grip on my psyche no longer held sway. I was released from captivity.

And then I got married at twenty; and reality reared up like an obstreperous stallion that did not want to be broken. I moved to Las Vegas and, for eighteen years, was confined to what I called the "third rung of hell."

Even before I received Carli's text message, I had been musing about my life in my sixth decade. I actually look back with nostalgia on the beautiful moment that November 11 day when I turned sixty. My oldest son, Jonathan, and his wife, Carli, gave me a splendid birthday party at the exquisite home of a friend with a very elegant newly built ballroom. I invited all the people in my life whom I loved dearly, my second son, Aaron, and his soon-to-be wife, Alyse, and people from yoga and tango.

Then, like an addict coming down off a high, I got home from my party and began a downward mental spiral. Reflecting on my night of birthday bliss, I hoped that I had sufficient fortitude to juggle future journeys and dreams. I simply wanted to keep dancing as if no one was watching. Given that my nature was not to censor myself or worry about what others were thinking, I was used to forging headlong into the pursuit of individual freedom and self-fulfillment. My ex-husband would call that being a hippie. My father would call it being eccentric ("asshole" followed "eccentric").

FUTURE PERFECT

What caught me up short was the realization that turning sixty-four meant that I had lived more than half my life. Panic set in: what were the next thirty years going to look like? I was compelled to put my mental house in order.

I was not particularly lonely; after all, my family was intact, albeit in Las Vegas. I still had a job, my aging mother was not well, and dementia had set in. I was a commuter grandmother. And yet, I was surprisingly uncomfortable with my life. The illusiveness of my mental malaise confused me. At sixty-four, I didn't feel my age; I had energy to spare, I prided myself on a positive attitude for life and adhered to the mantra of the Steely Dan song *Hey 19*. Nineteen was an age and a time when everything was possible and nothing stood in the way of what I wanted to do.

I started to think that if there are no field manuals to help me slug it out on in my sixties, no self-help books, and no curriculum, what's a sixty-four-year-old girl to do with all that angst and confusion? I'm not buying into the cliché that sixty is the new fifty. Face it: My skin had more elastin when I was fifty. Check out your arms and jawline in the women's dressing room at Nordstrom, and you'll get a dose of your real age. Those overhead lights can make anyone head for a plastic surgeon.

One of my dearest friends and yoga student, Corinne, said to me one day as I was again bemoaning being sixty-four and single,

"You're on the back nine, Joanie baby." At that moment, I felt as if I was seeing the white light. I mustered a mental return to earth and hoped that this decade would not be my last act. Maybe the back nine wasn't so bad. After all, I still had time to find balance and inner peace. In the meantime, being sixty-four seemed as oppressive as a summer day in Vegas.

It's obvious that I'm not a big fan of getting older. Who is? And I know that men, single or married, are not big fans of aging either. Men just talk about it less. Women may go off to a plastic surgeon to get a partial lift so no one will notice or sign up for a Botox party at 10 percent discount (hard to resist) and reenter the world, sporting the smile of a Cheshire cat. But a man searches for a younger woman to validate his testosterone levels. Problem solved! It's ubiquitous in a culture that is self-absorbed and somewhat (okay, a lot) narcissist to validate our youth. We don't have to constantly forage for food and shelter so we have the luxury of time to endlessly speculate on the aging process.

One of my dear friends and yoga clients, Kathy, is going through some of the fits and starts and surprising confusions of living in her sixties. Today we practiced yoga. Today we talked about how random and surreal our experiences seemed to be in our sixties. Sometimes we felt like visitors in our own families, and we were clueless about how to deal with our adult children. We were often called back to family responsibilities that we had not anticipated. While we were watching over our progeny, the dynamics were changing. We were different and we couldn't explain it.

More to the point, I was unable to find my authentic older woman's inner voice. I suspected that one of the reasons I was obsessively disappointed at my age was that my search for finding love again had positively eluded me. And if I found a life partner, was I going to catch the brass ring or find myself back to square one trying to sustain an unsustainable relationship?

On the other hand, I reasoned in more conscious moments that without a man in my life, I clearly had the opportunity to fully pursue my passions of yoga and tango, improve my mind, and devote more time to teaching and to exploring the inner connection to self without the conflicts and distractions inherent in a steady relationship.

I was perpetually conflicted about my topsy-turvy state of mind, and clear thinking was eluding me, causing some psychological setbacks. I didn't know what I was feeling. It was a challenge to stay focused as my unconscious emotional baggage floated to the surface.

Sometimes I just had to slap myself because I was more conscious about the state of my universe than I realized. I have always tried to remember that my spirits could be lifted with an intention to live an honorable and worthy life with an open heart and mind. After all, I am a yoga teacher and practice mindful meditation, the process of being present with experiences and emotions as they occur, actively paying attention to my thoughts, feelings, and bodily sensations.

But, let's face it: life can be a bumpy ride. I had a few regrets, I had loss, I had my individual struggles, and I had a few personal demons. Yet, I reasoned that if I didn't have pain, how could I recognize the joy? The yin and yang is ever present. "It's all good," says one of my yogi masters.

BRINGING IN THE SHEAVES

When my phone beeped and Carli's text showed up on the screen, I was eating dinner with my best male friend, Peter, at our favorite sushi restaurant in the Valley. We meet on most Saturday nights before we dance tango. It's a cherished ritual that neither one of us ever wants to give up. We talk about world politics, my failed relationships, my sons' continual need to parent me, mother complexes of men I have known, our respective acute indigestion issues, my ninety-six-year-old mother's declining health, my guilt over my brother being her caregiver, Peter's escapades in a moribund real estate market, and his constant assurance that he absolutely knows how we can achieve happiness and fulfillment because his real estate guru told him the secret. And, of course, the subtext of all this dialogue is about my attempt to age gracefully and keep my Berkeley cool in the midst of guilt, loss, and tepid feelings of loneliness. Peter, my partner in crime, feeds into the ravings of my redundant mind with aplomb.

I read Carli's text to Peter, and he howled with laughter at my daughter-in-law's message. I just love Peter because he gets "stuff" that women get. He's got no mother complex, no commitment issues, and is perfectly happy with his anima, his feminine side. Peter keeps telling me I have no relationship to being sixty-four and to please stay the nineteen-year-old I have always been.

INT. SUSHI RESTAURANT - NIGHT
JOAN and PETER drink sake and share sushi.

          PETER
This is really good sushi, darling. I can't get over how fresh it is.

          JOAN
     (smiling at Peter)
You're not listening to me.

          PETER
Yes, I am, darling. I've heard every word you said.

          JOAN
I'm saying I had no preparation for turning sixty.

          PETER
You're well over sixty, precious angel.

          JOAN
Not funny. It's crazy, but it's like this decade is an obstacle course, and I can't for the life of me get over the humps.

> PETER
> You mean "bumps," don't you, angel? You're probably right. But I wouldn't worry about it. You look like you're nineteen, and you act like you're nineteen; so although I hear your angst, I just don't get what the fuss is all about.

> JOAN
> It's a paralysis problem. I'm even feeling too old to dance tango.

> PETER
> Now that's bunk, precious angel.
> (points to a piece of sushi)
> Are you going to eat the shrimp? I will if you don't.

> JOAN
> Listen, darling, I've only got thirty good years left. And they are hardly going to be my golden years!

Peter is a year older than I am, British, and completely graceful as he moves through his life. He never gives aging much thought and always looks like a million bucks. He is the only hypochondriac I have ever adored. He does kvetching with charm.

"My stomach hurts, angel," Peter whines. "I really have a gastrointestinal issue, and it must come from those bloody Santa Ana winds."

After sushi, Peter and I drove to the dance studio. As we entered, tango music was playing. I placed my purse and wrap on our reserved seats, and Peter took my arm to guide me onto the dance floor. I couldn't move.

"Remember. Screw sixty-four," he said.

After years of learning tango from the best maestros in the world, dancing in Europe and South America and all over the United States, I wanted to run out of the *milonga* and hide somewhere in an alternative universe.

"Oh, darling, whatever are you thinking? You're my teacher, and you have to dance with me tonight," Peter said.

The scene suddenly didn't seem familiar or relevant. I, the eternal nineteen-year-old, suddenly thought I was too old to tango. Could it be that I was having a nervous breakdown or, worse, succumbing to stereotypes? I hate it when that happens!

I thought about what Corinne had said, about living large on the "back nine." The "back nine" involves chronology, and it was the concept of time that was screwing with my head. I should have been thinking about quantum physics. Time is only a continuum to help us mortals control, function, and organize our lives. Imagine how awkward it would be to live without a structured environment that is defined by calendar years and the place of the sun in the universe.

Perhaps I was fearful of going forward in time and coming up empty; or maybe I was searching for protection from isolation, loss, and loneliness. If I could only understand what was happening deep inside my unconscious, I could move into a moment when my soul was free again.

I smiled painfully and slowly took one step forward to find my balance and then cautiously moved onto the dance floor. I began to embrace the Zen of the moment, a moment that I love so much. I picked up the familiar smells of my partners, responded to brief snippets of dialogue about the musical selections, received nods to dance from my regulars, the go-to male dancers whose movements I know with my eyes closed. I began to dance as if no one was watching.

Maybe I was being a bit overdramatic with Peter, but it just didn't make sense that paralysis was setting in after all I have been through in my life. Granted I had always been a Pollyanna by nature, always forged ahead with crazy ideas, took leaps of faith, and seemed to land on my feet. I made decisions for my life that were not always logical or even sane because they ran counter to good judgment. However, I always had the luck of the Irish about me, and it never let me down.

ONE STEP FORWARD, TWO STEPS BACK

The first twenty years of my career was in theater. No one makes money in theater unless he or she is a star actor or director. I was neither, but money didn't seem to matter to me. I loved the theater and the movies from the time I was a child. I was a high school drama teacher in the late sixties with a salary of barely $6,000 a year, facing a daily landscape of pot-smoking, LSD-taking misfits. I lasted a year teaching high school. I went back to college, earned a master's degree in education, and then went back to teaching at my old high school for another three years. I returned to University of Nevada, Las Vegas, for another masters—this time in theater. I held a position as an acting and education instructor at UNLV for four years, and then I hit a snag.

Even though I had published two textbooks on acting and taught several acting classes and a stage movement class, I wasn't being given opportunities to direct on the main stage. I complained to the president of that august university that the theater department was a bastion of male chauvinism. The president, a biologist by profession, told me that if I wanted to do something more in theater, I should go off campus. Hello, glass ceiling; good-bye, academic pursuits.

I am woman; hear me roar. What does any liberated woman do in the seventies? She gives the guys in the theater department the finger and bravely goes out on her own. I cofounded an equity theater in a shopping center down the road from UNLV and became its artistic director. Everyone told me I was crazy. Who wants to go to an off-Strip theater when you've got the Las Vegas Strip? Ever heard of bingo? In spite of challenging economic times, the theater lasted five years. The fallout from my theater's eventual demise was that my marriage was also over.

ON THE ROAD

My single journey officially got started when I left Las Vegas with my two young sons in tow and drove out of the desert in my Toyota Supra heading toward the Pacific Ocean and San Diego. I was completely confident that water was the antidote to a failed marriage. I wasn't running away to San Diego so much as desiring to forge another journey. I had no idea what my life would look like; I had no vision what I was supposed to do or be. But I was in my late thirties, so jumping off a cliff without a net seemed perfectly logical. After putting the boys in school, I began work as a professional actress at the elite Old Globe Theatre with stints at dinner theaters in the hinterlands. Actors get paid just slightly better than domestic workers.

Two years later, my theater career was on its last leg. Both sons had chosen to live with their father, so I wandered up the coast to Los Angeles and enrolled at the American Film Institute, deducing correctly that my producing skills in theater were translatable to producing skills in film.

Leaving the theater was not as traumatic experience as it might have been since I didn't think playwrights were writing about the important societal or cultural themes during the 1980s. Movies were doing a better job of reflecting America's societal issues of the day. As plays became less vital and less interesting, actors were reduced to bloviating, babbling talking heads. Since most modern plays lacked a third act, there was little opportunity to lead the audience to an emotional climax or produce a conflict resolution. There wasn't much to talk about after the play at the neighborhood bar.

Furthermore, I decided my acting career was finished the year before when, after twenty-two years, I was still waiting for my entrance cue backstage. I was working at the Old Globe Theatre in San Diego, and my role was a simpering young woman dressed in the most appalling brown drab costume in an unbelievably boring play by a Hungarian playwright. I turned to the famous actress standing behind me, Marion Ross, Mrs. C on Happy Days.

"I'm tired of waiting for my cue, Marion," I said sadly.

With a wry smile, Marion replied casually, "Well then, darling, you don't have to do it anymore. You can do whatever you want in life."

Who knew it was that simple? The irony of the moment was not lost on me. Leave it to Mrs. C to give me my answer. I left the theater to do whatever it was I wanted to do in life.

For the next decade, I worked as a screenwriter. The monetary rewards were slim, but it was a wonderful, creative time in my life. Eventually, when I had to trash the antique computer, when it was crucial that I make a viable living and take care of two teenage sons, I still found work options and was free to choose a profession that interested me.

There was very little logic in the next leg of my journey. Since I had a Screen Actors Guild card and an Actors' Equity card, I became a movie/TV extra at the ripe age of fifty. When the Hollywood glitz wore off, I trained as an ESL (English as a second language) teacher and taught for six years in a language school. I worked with executives all over the world and met young students who thought English was their ticket to success in their countries of origin. It was an exciting and invigorating experience.

The years that I trolled for sustenance and budgeted money as exercises in self-mastery—finding joy in each day, in each job, in each encounter with another human being—were the best years of my life. My reward came to me when I discovered yoga in my midfifties. The idea that I would eventually teach didn't enter my mind until one day I quit or was fired from a brokerage house (I can't remember exactly which came first) and started teaching yoga at fifty-nine. It was a leap of faith and years of practice that naturally evolved into the teaching of yoga. I never forgot what my yoga guru said to me: "If you can stay present, you can follow your bliss."

When I look back on the several decades before arriving in my sixties, I sometimes I think it was someone else's life. It was a strange odyssey, randomly planned but fairly well executed once I landed on my feet. I suppose my father was right. I was eccentric in my own way. And my mother was right when she said I would always be a bohemian at heart. I always felt as if I rode the rails and jumped off the train when the spirit moved me. Embracing my life with love and passion proved to be the secret to creating personal joy, the most cherished and human of all emotions.

When I lived in San Diego, a female acquaintance once asked me, "What do you do?" At that moment, I didn't know what to say because I had no acting job—in fact, no job at all.

"I'm living my life," I simply responded.

Text message from David
Weenie, @ football practice
w/ Aaron, to Eric's 4 overnite
get wine & steaks get momantic

CHAPTER 2
GET RID OF THE SCRIPT

I met my significant other, David, the almost stepfather to my boys, at the American Film Institute. And my life was forever changed by his presence and love.

David started the producing program at AFI; and he was our guide, our teacher, our guru, and our king of all that related to film. Think of Ernest Hemingway in Spain going to bullfights and writing The Sun Also Rises. Think of the drama and feel of a bullring, and that was David. I instantly fell in love the moment I met him. Of course, he was handsome and sexy, but it was his mind and humor that turned me on. Even before I finished my first year as a producing fellow, we moved in together and became not only producing and writing partners but also partners in life.

David had been a longtime film producer and understood the vagaries of Hollywood better than most. He warned me that we would be regularly subjected to the whim of the Hollywood gods, and it wasn't going to be pretty.

In the mid-1980s, when we got together, the entertainment business was going through its usual muddy waters, especially with a writer's strike that was crippling to a good portion of writers and producers. David always said the entertainment business wasn't a business. That's an oxymoron if there ever was one. He had been a studio producer long enough to know that one day, you were in the club; and the next day, your office was packed up in a box, and you were booted out of the studio system without explanation.

It was tempting to live in the illusion of the future while waiting for our ship to dock, for our deals to come through, and we both succumbed to living off hopes and dreams. The real world wasn't always kind. The machinations of the movie industry too often infringed on our dreams and gave our relationship way too many time-outs.

David and I always made the best of what we had in life. While we gambled on our future, our alternative family unit was thriving. I bought a fixer house and then another and another at the height of the housing market. We strung together weekend potlucks with our neighbors, all the while sustaining a relationship that bound us together through the best and worst of times.

I was a writer for anyone who wanted to pay me. David taught producing at a variety of professional film schools. And we wrote screenplays by the pound and developed enough TV ideas to pitch one a day for a month. I wrote a novel on my fossilized word processor, lined my bathroom walls with rejection letters, bought another fixer, and lost my divorce settlement trying to keep two mortgages afloat in the downturn of a bad real estate market in the early 1990s. We went to dozens of football and basketball games, and I filled out more college applications and wrote more "why I want to go to your university" essays than I ever thought possible (why did each of my boys have to pick ten schools?). I went back to the Catholic Church for sanity and salvation and survived it all without regrets.

By the time I was an empty nester, I was exhausted and still couldn't rub two nickels together to make any money. So much for a secure financial future. Yet, in those days with David, it was always about the process of living and the fun and joy of creating the journey.

TANGO X TWO

In 1987, I got rid of my life's script. I saw a tango show called *Tango X Two*. I don't fully understand the process by which someone knows that he or she should take up golf, learn tennis, play the piano, or join a tap dancing group. I've been a creative person all my life, and my instincts are to be sensitive to artistry. The spoken word and performance had been my conduits for creative communication. Tango captured my imagination like nothing else since I left the theater. Its creativity comes from the uniqueness of the dance; it is an improvised conversation without words. Plácido Domingo once said that tango was a five-act opera.

The tango dancers I saw on stage were spellbinding, sensual, graceful, and athletic, with quiet torsos and rail-straight backs and feet that moved as fast as sound. Argentine tango does not have the heightened style of the American ballroom tango, which is about artifice and reflects the caricature of Rudolph Valentino in the 1920s movies. Argentine tango dancers express the passions and emotions of the music in subtler, more languid movements or in fast spurts of emotional expression. It was a dance of the street with a blend of indigenous and ethnic influences. Even though I was watching show tango, or *fantasia*, at the Pantages Theater, its essence was similar to the tango danced in the salons of Buenos Aires.

Tango and its music are compelling and addictive. The bandoneon, the instrument in tango that produces its haunting sound, punctured my soul. I later learned that tango music originated from Brazil and Cuba, from indigenous people in South America, with elements of German and Italian folklore.

After the show, I was stunned. The dancers left the stage but I was still watching.

```
INT. PANTAGES THEATER - NIGHT
JOAN and DAVID sit in the empty theater, staring at
the stage.

                    JOAN
          I'm going to learn to tango from
          every one of those maestros on-
          stage tonight, and I'm going to
          dance tango the way they do.

                    DAVID
          I knew you'd love it.
```

                    JOAN
How did you know about tango?

                    DAVID
I saw it in the social clubs in Buenos Aires and in remote places in the interior of Argentina.

                    JOAN
When you were in the CIA?

                    DAVID
Sure, they were dancing tango all over the place in the sixties until the junta. I used to see it all the time when I went to Argentina for R & R.

                    JOAN
Was it this sexy?

                    DAVID
It was earthy and very seductive. Tango was unsophisticated in those days. You have to remember that tango was first danced in the bordellos in Buenos Aires. Tango and its music weren't acceptable in society. Then tango came to Paris, and it was a hit. The rest is history.

How exciting that tango had such a wonderful history! I had to learn it. I had to find a way to dance tango before I died. David was always leading the way for me, inspiring me and taking me into the richest of places. There was no one more encouraging or intuitive than David.

After my youngest son went to college, I went in search of a tango class. And then I went to Buenos Aires to chase the tango, to dance with hundreds of milongueros. These are men, specifically, but women too who dance tango every night at the *milongas,* the salons where people gather to dance tango socially. I have danced tango for more than fifteen years, and I will continue to do so until I can no longer move my feet.

Almost sixteen years after I met David, through years of love and struggle, laughter and tears, we separated. I was fifty-nine. Our dance was over, but our connection would last forever in my heart. He will always be the most important man in my life.

DO YOU BELIEVE IN MAGIC?

It took courage to keep moving forward in life, and in the decade of my sixties without David by my side, the challenge was even greater. However, I had the opportunity to learn the most about myself than in any other decade. I surely wasn't going to get wisdom all of a sudden. But I had the chance to do some emotional and psychic healing, which might directly influence the quality of the rest of my life. It was like clearing out the old cobwebs in the attic of my mind. Maybe I could even get rid of the old scrapbooks with pictures of Joanie at nineteen and find out who Joanie was about to become.

Of course, I still had fears and anxieties about growing older. Yet, the irony was that as I began to write *60, Sex & Tango*, I learned that I am perfectly myself when I forget about age. I was in the process of understanding that it is not necessary to reinvent myself. It was more important to embrace my life and live my narrative story with a clear mind and an open heart. Writing also gave me the opportunity to study and select options for my life that were compatible to my needs: emotional, spiritual, mental, physical, sexual, parental.

The yogis say we are born with everything we need, all the happiness we can handle, all the joy that we would ever want in life. It's just that we screw it up as we go along through life. This is called struggle, and struggle is unnecessary and avoidable. Yet, the ego mind is powerful and unrelenting. It is responsible for creating conflict when it senses it needs protection, and that is most of the time. I always tell my yoga students, "Park your ego at the door." Hey, I didn't invent this stuff. Check out Eckhart Tolle and his best-selling book, *The Power of Now*, and his second best seller, *A New Earth: Awakening to Your Life's Purpose*, an in-depth analysis of the interplay of the ego mind and how it affects and drives our emotional well-being. We arrive on earth, and we are here and now.

DON'T DRINK THE KOOL-AID

The other night, I was sitting at the *milonga*, and a special woman friend scooted next to me. Our conversation naturally revolved around turning sixty. She said sadly to me, "I should do more with my life. I wonder if I still have time left to do the things I want to do." My friend has been a very successful television writer, but recent years have not produced what she considered success. Yet, she had succeeded in a business that would make most people envious. I remarked on her success running a dance studio with her partner, providing dance classes and *milongas* to the community. She was also a tango dancer and teacher and a light in our tango world.

"Count up all you have really accomplished in your life," I told her. "And you will find an abundance of a life well lived."

In order to move into the narrative of my story, to get through my personal paralysis, I decided to make some observations about myself and assess my present state of mind.

I made a list of things I never thought I would be doing at sixty-four:

I'm still dancing tango, but now with a sense of joyous freedom I never had before.

I'm still teaching yoga and enjoying it more than ever.

I have even more opportunities to teach yoga at UCLA.

I'm writing this book. It is sometimes scary.

I'm traveling alone for the first time. It is sometimes scary.

I'm planning more travel adventures alone. Next year, instead of my usual trek to Buenos Aires, I'm venturing out to Southern Spain and Morocco. This year, it was Costa Rica. Next, I'm going to Bali.

I splurged on myself and bought my first $100 lace Cosabella bra.

I'm in love with my four grandsons: Jordan, Luc, Greyson, and Jude and having the best time being a gran ("gran" is my moniker for "grandmother").

I'm actually having reasonable relationships with my two adult sons, Jonathan and Aaron. Sometimes it's rocky, but it's always filled with love and humor.

I'm dealing reasonably well with my ninety-six-year-old mother, who is almost completely bedridden, deaf, and afflicted with dementia.

I'm trying not to feel guilty that my brother is the major caretaker, along with his wonderful second wife, Pat.

I'm meditating daily.

I am a licensed drug counselor providing yoga and meditation to people in recovery.

I went back to therapy because my ever-supportive, ever-loving, and graceful friend Corinne suggested I see her Jungian therapist.

I have made the most incredible new female friends. They are also my yoga students who share individually and collectively in my life's narrative.

I rediscovered an old lover who is now and forever one of my best friends. There is such joy in finding an old shoe.

I'm learning to live alone. It's difficult and sometimes not pleasant, especially the part about cooking for one. It sucks!

I bought a MacBook. I swore I wouldn't be a Mac groupie. I am.

After several failed love affairs, I'm still hopelessly open to developing a new relationship with someone who just may be "the one" that enlarges and energizes both our lives.

I like lists. Lists are magical because they are the creation of my mind. They provide clarity and provoke questions. And lists make the present more real. It is surprising to realize how many gifts I give myself daily, monthly, and yearly. If sometimes lists annoy me, I write my thoughts in a journal. Journaling is therapeutic and cheaper than a shrink. Or better yet, write a book.

WHERE ANGELS FEAR TO TREAD

Carl Jung, one of the foremost psychologists and thinkers of the twentieth century, says that accepting our fears is the best place for healing to begin. My therapist, Mike, a Jungian psychologist, tells me to find the source of my fears in my dreams and befriend them. Befriend them? It took me a while to wrap myself around that concept.

I understand, however, that living in fear produces negative thoughts and emotions that mask the larger truths of my life. That means I'm living in half-light and shadows and can't get into the meat and potatoes of my being. I can't possibly live in the present when I am fearful that the worst is going to happen in the future. Future thinking can sometimes frustrate me because it is not the here and now. I might get angry and disregard my innate goodness. As a result of this mental construct, my positive energy dissipates.

Dream analysis helped me reflect on unconscious fears that I avoided examining. Scientists who research the brain postulate that certain people are predisposed to excessive fears that originate from our environment. It's not necessarily a bad thing to be afraid. In fact, one of the ego's functions is to keep fears active. The ego tells us "fearing is for our own protection." Being fearful will keep us free from harm. On the other hand, remarking about imagined fears, Mark Twain said, "I have been through some terrible things in my life, some of which actually happened."

Nevertheless, it's unhealthy for fears to take over my life because I know I'm inevitably going to miss the best moments of love and creativity if I focus on fear and anxiety. I'm going to miss the sublime moments of dancing tango and inspiring teaching. I'm going to miss the colors of being a grandmother. I want to renew daily my commitment to facing my fears with courage and gratitude so I'll have space for growth and transformation.

I studied a little Eastern philosophy; and when I compare the Eastern sensibility with Western thought, I am perplexed that one of the central beliefs of Western culture fosters a self-serving, self-involved perspective. The Western ideal encourages my need to belong and to be loved all the time. I don't like the idea that I must live up to other people's standards. That's an impossible order; it requires self-monitoring and puts me in a mental hammerlock that takes me out of the present and roots me in future thought or past memories. I want to act without the push and pull of Westernized convention.

What I do, if I can remember, is to take a step back from myself and do what the yogis do: Act by setting small intentions. Working from intentions keeps me in the present and guides me through fears and excessive neediness. Goals serve our future needs, the long-distance planning that gets us our PhD or that job we always wanted researching diabetes. Goals are guides for the future, and if I live completely inside those goals, I will create excessive tension and stress. It is so much easier if I keep grounded in reality by setting daily, even hourly, intentions.

Sometimes when I feel afraid, I call to mind my list of intentions:

When I feel afraid, I stop my physical and mental activity and breathe along with the fear. Better yet, I try to embrace the fear.

I try to find a name for the fear.

I try to create a larger context for the fear by relating the fear to the divine wholeness of my life.

I try to blend my fear with a sense of compassion for myself.

If overwhelmed, I do something physical, such as take a walk or call a friend or listen to my favorite music or dance around the house as if no one is watching.

I breathe deeply to keep energy flowing.

I meditate to manage stress and anxiety.

Making a list of fears is not easy. It takes courage to say them out loud and fortitude to write them down. Mental gridlock is a bitch. It leaves me enervated. Releasing my fears allows me to grow and transform.

No matter the decade, I know enough to expect the unexpected. I know that I'm going to live with struggle, yet I don't know the exact nature of my struggle, and that is a good thing. After all is said and done, my life is a mystery to be unraveled, moment by moment. I can solve the mystery if I put aside the inauthentic struggles and direct my focus inward through meditation; and in doing so, I might reveal a thousand parts of my mind that I have yet uncovered.

This is the power of now. This is the way to follow my bliss. This is my real job. This is this.

Text message from my son Jonathan
not going to b in Vegas
4 Thanksgiving
taking boys to Philly...
make plans w/
Aaron if u want

CHAPTER 3
YOUR CHILDREN ARE GROWN, GET OVER IT

I would love to get over my children, but I can't. They're my children. My adult children. Having children is painful and joyful at the same time. Parental love: it's a minefield of conflicting emotions and there is no turning back. Dr. Phil, Deepak Chopra and Oprah, our twenty-first-century spiritual gurus, have been ruminating, philosophizing and running amok for decades about all aspects of love, particularly parental. Let's face it—no one knows anything about anything, and if they think they do, they are people you don't want to be around. All I can postulate is that finding and achieving balance between parent and child is the toughest aspect of parental love.

Since I have sons, I am parenting from the female/mother point of view with its own subset of psychological and emotional constructs. I don't have daughters, but I am a daughter, and I know the parental narrative is different between daughters and their mothers. I remember reading Nancy Friday's My Mother, My Self, with a sense of relief that I wasn't the only daughter whose relationship with her mother was complex and often subliminally dysfunctional.

But the male gender—they are always so, well, male; and I don't understand my sons any more than I understand the man I married, the men I've loved, or the men I've dated and hated. Discussing my sons and my energetic relationship with them poses considerable consternation, frequent high anxiety, and piles of my Catholic/

Jewish guilt. How did they get to be all grown-up without me? The deep cavern that lies between childhood and adulthood is a mystery. I'm at a loss about what actually transpired. I'm often nostalgic when I see them, as if they were fluffy teddy bears needing a cuddle. Most of the time, I vacillate between my need to stay attached to them and their need to maintain distance.

Sometimes I can't even talk to my adult children. Sometimes I talk to them, and we get off on the wrong foot. Then no one listens. If I could possibly put my ego aside and adhere to a list of meaningful communication skills with my adult children, then, perhaps, I could forge a permanent balanced relationship. It might look like

Love
Honesty
Trust
 Respect
Listening
Courtesy

I'm not a therapist. I don't know what is excessive and what is in the normal range of emotional healthy parent-child love. It is completely inappropriate for me to make judgments about other parent-child relationships. All I know is that I made some good decisions and some bad decisions raising my boys, and it is the present that I am concerned with now.

How do I negotiate getting my needs met as a mother and a grandmother, and how do my sons balance their relationship with Mom without getting overly involved?

I consult my friends frequently for guidance on this subject, and there are no really good answers except to keep my mouth shut. Zip it! My friend Kathy tells me she lives in fear of opening her mouth and saying something that could start another round of adult-child disconnect. The adult children can turn on an emotional dime for who knows what reasons, and the parent can find herself or himself in purgatory.

"I'm not coming to your house for Christmas this year," said Kathy's daughter. "We are going to our friend's house."

Translation: you are not important this Christmas, Mom. We all have our Christmas stories, I'm sure. After my last holiday catastrophe last winter, I'm plumb out of ideas for creative, harmonic convergence with adult children.

CHANGING THE URBAN FLOOR PLAN

My children are grown, and they have moved on! I consider myself lucky because some children do not move on. I've heard of daughters so attached to their mothers they have to call every day and tell them everything. Their closeness becomes a dependency, beyond the range of normal parental love for both mother and daughter. I had no further desire to cuddle with my mother after I left home for college. On the other hand, Latin men, especially the Argentine men, lavishly adore Mama; and it's not a pretty sight.

When parents and children feed into each other's dependency and call it love, no child has the opportunity to individuate, and parents don't develop the skills to transition to the next phase of their lives. Some adult children return home after college or decide to move back home even though they are in the workforce, thereby extending their familial dependency. Or in some cultures, particularly in Italy, it is extremely common for boys not to leave home until they are married. It often takes the male well into his thirties to find a bride. Home is just too comfortable with Mama meeting all the needs of her son. It's not so easy to leave a home that serves Mama's homemade pasta every night. Thank God, I'm not a very good cook.

Parents who let their adult children return for extended periods of time find themselves either having to keep their big house instead of downsizing or rearranging the floor plan to make room for their twenty-seven-year-old son who decides to quit his job because the corporate world is stifling his inner artist. This isn't going to work for me because I have a one-bedroom apartment. Sometimes by changing the urban floor plan, parents might find that they might have unduly fostered a son's or daughter's inner child instead. Of course, there are always extenuating circumstances that can cause an adult child to return home, like a huge economic downturn resulting in a prolonged recession. Now, that's a problem.

There is a chance that adult children moving back home might create confusion inside the household. The once-defined relationship boundaries between parent and child may shift, and there could be a reversion to the old parent-child dependence model. There could be a loss of freedom for all concerned. The important point here is to be mindful of the adult children's dependencies so that, at appropriate intervals, the parents can encourage a transition back into the world. Or kick them out altogether. But what do I know? My sons knew better than to move back in with me.

READING TEA LEAVES OR HOW ANCESTOR WORSHIP FELL INTO DISREPUTE

There is one thing I am certain of as a parent of adult children. My adult children will in some manner feel the need to confront me no matter my age. As a so-called mature adult, I am accountable for my actions and words. But I am human. I am fallible. I have foibles. I lapse into unconscious emotional responses as my raging ego protects and defends me when I am attacked. But I want these confrontations with my sons to be less and less of a burden to all of us.

I've actually learned a few things since both my sons married and created their own families. Above all else, I think it's important to have a clear and specific intention when communicating with my adult children. I must phrase everything gently and carefully so that there is no cause for being defensive. If I don't have a clear intention, I find it helpful if I take some time to assess the dynamics of the problem and put my perceptions of the situation on hold. I say this with a straight face, knowing that I've mishandled communication with my sons too many times to count. Or, I could take a Valium.

Recently, an incident occurred at my youngest son's home that illustrates a vintage child-parenting moment. I was visiting my third grandson, Greyson, as I had been doing once a week since he was born.

INT. AARON'S KITCHEN - DAY

AARON and JOAN are in the kitchen. Joan is getting ready to leave the house.

                AARON

You left the teacup on the counter, and you didn't wash it.

                JOAN

I was rushing out. I usually clean up.

                AARON

Why do you keep doing your laundry here? It's getting to be a habit.

                JOAN

I've only done it twice, and that's because I wanted to spend more time with the baby.

                AARON

You're sure it's not because you're a little cheap? It's weird.

                JOAN

It's only a dollar at my building.

                AARON

And if you want food, you should ask.

                JOAN

You told me to eat anything I want.

> AARON
> You don't always say thank you.
>
> JOAN
> What's this about, Aaron?
>
> AARON
> You overstep boundaries, Mom.

I bounced from 1 to 100 in three seconds on the anger scale and then went blind and deaf, and I should have gone dumb but didn't. For all the times I cleaned up, watched the dogs, house-sat, folded their laundry, why did I have to give excuses for ordinary behavior? I stomped out of the house. Just as I got to the door, I heard, "Way to communicate, Mom! Just get angry and leave." It wasn't my finest moment, yet it wasn't my worst either.

My sons are not slavishly devoted to me. It would be nice if they were slightly more respectful, but I know it is important for their mental and emotional health to keep an appropriate set of personal boundaries. However, sometimes those boundaries are perceptions rather than real issues.

I have come to realize over these formidable growth years that Jonathan and Aaron have personal agendas concerning me, and I don't necessarily know what they are about. While my sons are not particularly demonstrative, I know they love and respect me in an above-average fashion. My sons sometimes ask me for advice or for an opinion, but they don't revere me. Ancestor worship is something the Chinese invented before they were born. My sons don't adhere to elderly wisdom.

Lately, the relational aspect has been more open with the birth of their children. I'm Gran now, and they are really proud of that aspect of our relationship. They put up with my idiosyncratic activities like tango dancing but think my work as a yoga instructor is awesome. Points of contention occur when they think I give them too much information or think I am judging. "Keep it short, Mom. Speak in bullet points." They tease me and joke around about my loser boyfriends, and they overscrutinize my life. However, my boys know that I'm available to lend unconditional emotional support.

These light moments are reality checks and balances that enable Jonathan and Aaron to move on from difficult moments because they know that I deeply care for their well-being and that I am present to listen. Just the other day, out of the blue, Jonathan called with good news to share. These are the moments I cherish with my sons, and they remind me to make more space for the ever-changing parent-child dynamics that are altering the landscape of our relationship.

On a cautionary note, when my sons are not getting along, I think it is crucial not to take sides. I put duct tape over my mouth or take a long trip or disconnect the phone. However, no matter how hard I try to stay out of their arguments, each one wants to draw me into their rants as they convince themselves that I am taking the other's side. Didn't this happen when they were seven and ten? Sibling arguments are a minefield of parental frustration, and they seem to be ubiquitous.

THE WANDERING JEWESS

Granted Jonathan and Aaron turned out great in spite of my flailing through decades of child rearing. And I'm incredibly delighted and proud of the way they grew into accomplished men. The boys have great values and terrific work ethics; they are smart, responsible, and, most importantly, honorable. They dutifully went to Hebrew school and became quasi-observant Jews, even though I was raised a Catholic. Confused yet? Don't worry. This story isn't a real stretch. When I was nineteen, my mother had the following conversation with me:

INT. JOAN'S BEDROOM, 1963 - MORNING
Joan's MOTHER is sitting on her bed. JOAN is reclining.

>MOTHER
>I just thought I'd tell you that
>your grandmother is Jewish.

JOAN
(calmly)
Oh, so what does that make you?

MOTHER
Nothing. I'm not anything.

JOAN
I thought you were Protestant.

MOTHER
I just put that on my job applications so I could get a job. It was easier for me.

JOAN
Grandma Rose is Jewish, and you're not? How does that work out?

MOTHER
I married your father, and he was Catholic. I met him at a YMCA dance. That's it. I don't have a religion.

JOAN
Why are you telling me this now? What difference could it possibly make to me?

MOTHER
You're dating a Jewish man, and I thought you should know.

Even before I knew I was a Jewess, I started to think I might be Jewish when I enrolled at UCLA. And this was a paradoxical notion because I grew up in a Catholic community so devoted to Catholicism that St. Raphael's Catholic Church was literally the center of town. Father Junipero Serra founded a mission on this land, and it was San Rafael's most cherished edifice. My options growing up in my sleepy, conservative, close-minded Catholic world were limited. Thank God for the great writers that lined the shelves in my mother's library: Tolstoy, Dostoyevsky, Hemingway, and Faulkner. These great writers gave me hope that there was another world outside my own cloistered convent world. Over time these great books would engage and excite my sensibilities.

I grew up with Irish and Italian kids. I knew one Jewish girl through my best friend in elementary school. However, it was only whispered that she was a Jew, like some exotic stripper that wasn't allowed to join the Catholic Women's League. Then there was a Goldberg, who attended my Catholic high school, and he was quite an oddity. No one ever mentioned that he was different from us because he went to church, and we thought he was a convert, and those people make the best Catholics. Because Goldberg was really cute, we were curious. What did it mean to be a Jew? We knew a Jew was a person from the Old Testament, which we never read; but we all knew that Jesus was a Jew, and Jews existed once upon a time in the land called Palestine. But, I mean, what really was a Jew?

I found out my first semester at UCLA. My first love was the son of a cantor who wouldn't take my virginity even though I begged him to. Now that's religion! He told me Jews don't believe that Jesus was the Messiah. I felt rejected and joined the Newman Center (Catholic group on campus), but everything lacked flavor after the adorable cantor's son taught me how to make soup that lasted for weeks and introduced me to my first Yiddish words. I felt strongly that I found my Jewish roots and a new cuisine, but I was insecure. Where was my bas mitzvah? Later, whenever I asked the random rabbi about whether I was a Jewess or not, the only answer was, "What, are you nuts? You're Jewish!" Please don't tell my mother or the pope.

I took dating a Jew one step further. I married a Jew and made sure my boys had a Jewish education just to right the spiritual confluences in the family tree. I call that poetic justice or keeping the generations on track or, more to the point, making it up as I go along. Funny, my mother never mentioned the subject again until Jonathan's bar mitzvah. Something about not liking the yarmulke on his head. That's what I call deep denial or pitch-perfect assimilation.

The irony was that my ex-husband considered himself a cultural Jew and not religious. The religious issues didn't come up until I was pregnant.

INT. JOAN AND HER EX-HUSBAND'S BEDROOM-MORNING
Joan's EX-HUSBAND is lying in bed. JOAN is getting ready for church. She is pregnant.

>   EX-HUSBAND
> Where are you going?
>
>   JOAN
> You know where I'm going. Do you have a couple of bucks?
>
>   EX-HUSBAND
> What for?
>
>   JOAN
> The collection basket. I need some dollars.
>
>   EX-HUSBAND
> I'm not giving a damn thing to the church. Use your own money.

>   JOAN
> Your money's my money. Anyway
> it's not hurting you. Oh, never
> mind.
>
>   EX-HUSBAND
> You're not going to raise the kid
> Catholic?
>
>   JOAN
> Never even considered it, sweet-
> heart.
>
>   EX-HUSBAND
> Don't take the kid to church.
>
>   JOAN
> Wouldn't even think about it,
> sweetheart.
>
>   EX-HUSBAND
> I don't know how a smart woman
> like you can be a Catholic. How
> can you buy that crap?
>
>   JOAN
> Habit, sweetheart.

To my consternation, since my ex-husband was neutral on the values of a Jewish religious education, I, the fledging Jewess, was out there on my own when it came to deciding my children's religious options. I was the one who decided to put my boys in Hebrew school in Las Vegas.

Turns out I was more of a Jew than he was. The Jewish community was welcoming and embracing; and besides, all my friends were Jewish, and their children all went to Hebrew school at the one temple in town. And so it was that I learned from my friends and my environment how to raise my boys in the Jewish religion. Judaism gave our family a spiritual connection and further bonded me with my sons. The irony is that Aaron still calls me a Catholic, but Jonathan takes me to High Holiday services. There you go.

ON THE WAY TO THE HOLY GRAIL

My two sons turned out much better than average. They are loving husbands and fathers. Neither of them had difficulty growing into men, falling in love, and committing to a woman. How random is that for a man? Men, and I've met more than my fair share, often struggle for a lifetime with what Carl Jung (the brilliant twentieth-century psychologist/philosopher) calls "eternal youth," or *puer* aeternus. I'm referring to men who resist transitioning into adulthood. We have all witnessed adult males who still play video games, roam unconsciously through their marriages and jobs, and pay lip service to raising their children. The kids are growing up, the wife has emotionally disconnected, and these men are still playing with their adult toys and chasing status symbols of wealth and/or sex. The *puers* don't notice the world changing around them. They're like kids on a sugar high.

Jung writes that man's unconscious state, his inability to fall in love, is a reflection of his mother complex. This complex does not necessarily mean that the man is replacing a love for a woman with his love for his mother, although it could, and then the man would be called a mamma's boy. However, the complex relates more to a man demonstrating an inability to come to terms with the opposite of the masculine, which is the relational feminine component, or the soul, called the anima.

The *mother complex* has its roots in mythology: The *puers* spend their entire lives fighting battles and slaying dragons, on the way to the Holy Grail, where they believe they will rescue the fair maiden in distress and find eternal happiness. But they never reach their fantasy woman (their feminine component) because the illusive "she" is an illusion, a creation of the man's imagination.

Since the fantasy woman is unattainable, the male never has to fall in love. It may look like the man has the ability to love because he may practice serial monogamy with a wife or girlfriend, but his heart is not actually open to a loving commitment. Unfortunately, for a woman, a man's inability to commit to a long-term loving relationship in or out of marriage usually ends very, very badly for the woman. It's difficult for relational females to concede that a man cannot love them completely for the duration of the marriage or the relationship. Unfortunately, this is one of the female's tragic flaws, along with forgetting their self-worth.

THANK YOU, DR. FREUD

I take absolutely no credit for my sons possessing a decent balance of masculine/feminine aspects. I don't know what I did or didn't do to encourage them to have a healthy sense of self as teenagers. Short of loving and encouraging them at every instance, there was no magical formula. They seemed to possess a natural understanding of the earthbound woman; after all, their mother made no bones that she was not a damsel in distress. Secretly, I suspect that my sons' affection toward me fell somewhere between Peg Bundy, the dysfunctional mother on *Married with Children,* and the Greek goddess Medusa, snakes and all.

As my sons grew older, they saw me as the prototypical flawed mother, and it became more difficult to decode our emotional connections. I'd like to imagine that they possessed an unconscious understanding of the mother archetype, which exists in all mythology. This mythological mother engenders devotion in an unconscious collective sense as intuited by all males. Nonetheless, the boys were often critical of me because they found cracks in my mothering/parenting style, maybe even defects in my character.

I seriously came up short as a mother for about ten years, and as a result, our relations lacked real interpersonal connection. The boys grappled emotionally with their unconscious fears of abandonment and projected their anger onto me because of the divorce, which often resulted in extremes of unbalanced energy.

I don't want to give this topic short shrift; however, my situation probably exemplified normal family dysfunction, as well as a smattering of Dr. Freud's Oedipal theory. I am sure there were unconscious sexual feelings that will never be addressed because you know how badly Oedipus behaved when he fell in love with his mother. Reminder: he killed his father and then blinded himself. Not exactly a model family in any century.

I'M DANCING AS FAST AS I CAN

Hindsight is an exact science. Sometimes reexamining a past decision is a cringing experience. It appeared I went a little over the top when, eighteen years to the day I arrived in Las Vegas, filled with fear and loathing, I packed my two boys into my Toyota Supra in the dead heat of the summer of 1982 and left town still full of fear and loathing. I told them about my plan a year ahead of time, but time means nothing to kids.

When I look back on that audacious move and the way I uprooted them, I feel nauseous. I justified my flight out of town because I had to stop a runaway nervous breakdown caused by fifteen and a half years of a marriage that was not conducive for my personal growth, my mother's need to have a coenabler by her side as she enabled my alcoholic father, and a career that I felt was about to implode.

Parental dysfunctions were difficult for my sons to endure. It wasn't easy going back and forth—from mother to father—from Las Vegas to San Diego, to Los Angeles, to Las Vegas. On Mother's Day almost two years after we arrived in La Jolla, my ex announced to me that his sons were going to live with him in Las Vegas. They left La Jolla and a really good Jewish school, and I moved to Los Angeles under the pretense that I was going to follow a career path.

I cried every day on the phone to my mother who had no sympathy. Her response was to the point.

INT. JOAN'S APARTMENT - MORNING
INTERCUT JOAN on the phone with her MOTHER.

> MOTHER
> You left your marriage. Now, you're paying the price. We don't get divorced in our family.

> JOAN
> What about Grandma? She got divorced twice. And what about Auntie? She was divorced three times. Why are you punishing me?

> MOTHER
> Work things out, Joanie.

> JOAN
> It's too late for that.

> MOTHER
> A wife should stay with her husband. Now you have to work for the rest of your life. What are you going to do?

> JOAN
> I'll find something, Mom.

> MOTHER
> And you even gave up acting in San Diego! Imagine. The Old Globe Theatre!

I didn't have much of a plan that first year in Los Angeles. In the mid-1980s, Los Angeles was a spaced-out city, a place where values no longer existed and where people careened out of control on cocaine. That first year was a blur and a whirl of late nights. Only the morning aerobics class at Jane Fonda's Workout Studio on Robertson Boulevard gave me a sense of community even though I never made a friend or spoke to anyone. It was a perfect trendy LA hot spot: sad and lonely. The entire year pained me deeply. Every time my sons came to visit me and slept on the futon, I felt emotionally bleached and spiritually lost.

It seemed I still had some Irish luck left. The American Film Institute graciously accepted me as a producing fellow based on a music video I produced. Then, nine months to the day that my sons left me, they arrived back in Los Angeles in a moving van with their beds. I was happy to have my sons back, but life soon became chaotic because once again I became the absent mom. Film school was as demanding as being an actress. I had to produce a slate of three films and go to school full-time.

Then a mystery befell me. I fell in love with my producing teacher (oh no, not falling in love with your teacher!), and I knew I deserved to die. The challenge of being a single parent with an adversarial relationship with my ex-husband, trying to start a new career in film, and falling in love with a man who was a complete stranger to my sons was overwhelming. Or maybe it was a plot from an Ibsen play.

The mother, possessed with powers for good and evil, chose evil and sabotaged the conventional, white picket fence family unit. A darkness descended on all.

The situation was ridiculously dysfunctional. And I was the adult!

ALL IN THE FAMILY
Returning into the fold of their mother and her new boyfriend/live-in was even more of an emotional upheaval in my son's lives. Today my sons can quote chapter and verse about my failings as a mother, but they can also recount my steadfast commitment to

their education and my constant love and support. I got points for letting them listen to Howard Stern in the mornings on the way to school so they could expand their conversational skills on topics like sex, drugs, politics, comedy, and pop psychology. (Stern still rocks for them and for me.) David and I never missed a game, a parent night, or gatherings with other parents. We provided a fun and stable atmosphere at home. I was determined Aaron was going to get his *Leave It to Beaver* family, even if it seemed more like Young Frankenstein's research lab. They also saw us continue to write and produce in the face of unending obstacles and adverse rejections. There were lessons learned in this environment that bore fruit later in their adult lives.

WHEN A PARENT BECOMES THE CHILD

I never wanted to hold on to my children. I remember thinking very early in their development that I wanted to raise them to be independent adults with a strong sense of self. Both boys made decisions early on about their life choices and took responsibility for their actions. They attended universities, traveled, chose their professions, and fell in love with women who would bring them joy and give them children. In the blink of an eye, I was on the other side of parenthood. Or so I thought. A little voice inside of my head kept warning me, "Not so fast, Joanie."

How does a parent become the child? We don't exactly say to them, "Go ahead and run my life now. I'm incapable, and I haven't done a great job of it as you can see. I can't make a living, and I'm practically living on the streets." I was not in any kind of compromising circumstances.

It began when David and I separated. Jonathan was really angry with me for ending my relationship with him because he was afraid that I would be alone and not have a protector. I cautioned my sons off and on for several years that David and I were not going to be able to stay together. It was past the time when we needed to go our separate ways. Love, respect, honor, history, loyalty, and devotion always got in the way of making the final decision. Jonathan and

Aaron wanted me to stay with David no matter the terms. It was another parental separation.

Leaving David was the first of many decisions I made that my boys didn't particularly agree with. I realized that, as I was trying to let them go, they were reversing roles. Just when I was beginning to feel my independence and make stupid mistakes all over again, I was being judged. I felt like a teenager again.

Then, when the boys began to live with their eventual spouses, I got lectures on boundaries. Jonathan would give me a key to his apartment, but I couldn't use it. I was invited to a party but had to leave when he told me I had to go. I started to date. Jonathan didn't like the guy I was going out with and wouldn't meet him for a drink, saying he didn't get a good vibe. Sure, he was a rebound, but he was a respectable rebound. Then, the rebound broke up with me.

"See, I told you he was no good!" Jonathan said to me with admonishing tone of a parent who is at his wit's end.

A psychic once told me that I was married to Jonathan in a former life. I think I believe it. Sometimes I know intuitively that we had a past connection because there are moments when lightning hits and the paranormal surfaces. My sons want to see me happy, but they also want to protect me from making mistakes along the way. Maybe they felt I failed; maybe they felt I should have stayed with their father. I should have made it work with David. Maybe those are my projections.

The worst thing I did was to try to explain that when relationships end, the result is not necessarily a failure. Any defense offered, any reasoned logic would provoke counterarguments. I was reduced to the child defending myself, and there was no meeting of the minds. As they matured, my sons developed their own perceptions of right and wrong regarding Mom. To this day, both of them tell me that I pick loser men and poor partners in business and that I probably should hire a life coach.

"Mom, next time, listen to me and pick a guy who treats you better," Jonathan barked at me like a priest in the confessional box giving out a penance.

The rebound didn't treat me badly. He just broke up with me and then treated me badly. And what do you mean "pick"? I get to pick a guy? I actually have a choice about who is going to be my life companion at sixty-four? Are they crazy? Oh yeah, the men are forming a queue outside my apartment. The real tragedy was that my rebound was a tango dancer. It was a bitter loss.

Confrontations between my sons and myself were direct, predicated on my sons' own personal agendas and their perceived interference by Mom.

"Mom, you shouldn't take a job in La Jolla and have to commute," Aaron opined because he didn't want me to leave David in Los Angeles by himself.

Wait! That's my livelihood. When could I get a job with that kind of pay, benefits, and good hours? Sure, the drive was two and a half hours, but I only drove that route once a week, and that was before gas was $4 a gallon. Any fool would have taken the job because it had the best view of the La Jolla Cove.

Before Jonathan was married to Carli, he broke up with her and decided to go back to his previous girlfriend. Trying to parent my son, I suggested he take a little longer to think about it. Mothers always try to protect their young.

"Mom, don't parent me! I know what I'm doing. I know you don't like her, so

don't say anything. Try to get along with her. She really likes you."

She never liked me. We never hit it off. Then, when he finally did break up with her two months later, it took Jonathan six months to get Carli back. I learned that in matters of the heart, it's best to stay neutral.

When Aaron temporarily moved his girlfriend into his cottage, I was concerned. I knew I was on thin ice because I was long past telling him what to do.

"It's just for a month or two until she finds another place," Aaron responded defensively. "She's living in a dump. Besides, what does it matter? I really like her."

She never moved out, and they eventually married. What did I know?

It seemed my boys didn't need me as mother protector after all. They were out in the world making their own mistakes, and they didn't need me to remind them that I once had parental rights. It became apparent that I needed to disengage from their lives in a healthy way. Support, yes. Prying, no. Practicing the art of detachment kept me out of volatile emotional arenas. It wasn't easy.

"That's what happens," Jonathan said to me. "You start as a child, and you end as a child."

Is that wisdom or just being a know-it-all?

I wouldn't have dared talk to my parents with such directness. I paid deference to my parents even when I felt they were wrong. However, my therapist pointed out that there were other influences on my sons—in particular, their father's tone and style of communication and his unconscious negative feelings about me. With time and a deeper understanding of both parents, my sons have somewhat resolved some of their parental issues. Or maybe I'm dreaming. Or maybe I'm projecting again because there was more drama ahead.

THE WEDDING CRASHER

It might be a cliché that weddings can bring out the best and worst in people, but in my case, it was true. The best of me came out with Jonathan's wedding. The worst of me came out in Aaron's wedding. I was the mother of the groom twice. That title has overtones of second-class status.

Aaron and Alyse put together their own wedding. My responsibility was to show up. I wish I had Aaron's wedding day back. I wish it hadn't played out like a Greek tragedy. Bringing my boyfriend at the time didn't help matters, especially one who had an adversarial relationship with my son, the groom.

I found out on the day of the wedding that Aaron and Alyse had not planned for me to speak at the wedding dinner. I was stunned and angry. When my ex-husband delivered his twenty-minute rambling monologue at the reception, he made an offhand derogatory comment about me. I crashed emotionally. Then Aaron gave his speech, and there was no recognition of a mother, either my son's mother or his bride's mother. I lost my composure. I looked over at my boyfriend, who was more livid than I, and left the room—my date following behind, eagerly fanning the flames of anger as if we were in *The Godfather* movie. Of course, he was Sicilian and looking for a fight.

Somewhere at the end of the speech, I heard from supporters that Aaron thanked me, but not before I had taken refuge on the beach and bummed a cigarette from a total stranger.

There was no deus ex machina to save the moment. That only happens in a Greek play when there is no way to resolve the situation. There was no god or goddess to come down from the heavens to save me. There was nowhere to run and nowhere to hide. The empress had no clothes! I cried the entire night, and the next morning, I felt like the walking dead.

My relationship with my adult children was in shambles. Their parenting of me turned into tough love. It was time to start therapy.

Text message from my son Aaron
Not going 2 talk until u apologize; alyse upset
u ruined our wedding

CHAPTER 4
BACK TO THERAPY: MI VIDA LOCA

Carli, my daughter-in-law, told me she was really proud of me for going back to therapy. Of course, she is a psychologist, and she is going to say that to me no matter what meshugaas happened at the wedding. Carli is my biggest fan, so you can imagine how soothing it was to have one ally in the family. I was sixty-two years old and conscious enough to realize that I needed some kind of help. It was probably a little late to start the maturation process, but therapy was my only option.

INT. CARLI'S KITCHEN, LAS VEGAS - DAY
JOAN and CARLI are drinking wine in the kitchen.

> CARLI
> It takes guts to go back to therapy at your age.

> JOAN
> I have no choice, do I? I have to find out what's going on with me and the rest of my world.

> CARLI
> Who's your therapist? I can recommend one in LA if you want.

JOAN
It's Corinne's therapist. He's a Jungian.

CARLI
Wasn't your last one Jungian? Why don't you go back to her?

JOAN
(slightly defensive)
I want a male this time.

CARLI
Are you sure you want a male therapist?

JOAN
He comes highly recommended. Corinne's been seeing him for twenty years.

CARLI
(jumps on it)
Twenty years?
(a long pause)
That's a long time to be going to therapy. Are you sure you'll be comfortable?

JOAN
Who better than a man to explain men to me? Besides, I don't want to work the cognitive behavior models. I prefer inner work, you know, digging into the psyche. I don't think Corinne goes to Mike

to be cured of anything specific. Working with Mike is about being conscious.

CARLI
He sounds unique.

I was rattling on. I didn't really know why I was going to Mike other than I liked Jungian analysis. But the truth was that the wedding incident shook me to my core.

"Of course, any kind of therapy encourages inner growth ...," Carli trailed off.

We yogis and professional therapists throw around words like "growth," "transformation," "mindfulness," "staying present," "raising the level of consciousness," "self-mastery" and expect everyone to understand what we mean by these concepts. I don't even understand all of this, let alone apply it consistently. I'm just someone who searches for inner peace and acceptance by practicing meditation. I find it quiets my mind and stills my body and eventually reduces stress and anxiety.

Evidently, personal growth and inner peace had little influence on my behavior. I got into trouble, and I ruined the wedding—at least that's what my adult children told me. Speculating that it was true, why go to all the effort to sign up for therapy? I'm smart. I can figure it out. Just find out what was going on, have a little talk, find out who did what to whom and why, and be done with it.

However, it was obvious that when the newly married couple returned from their honeymoon, nothing was forgotten or forgiven. Their silence was deadly. Then came the angry, unproductive phone calls. White noise filled the phone lines. We switched to e-mails, which turned into rants. There were text messages, which went unanswered because I refused to learn texting.

It occurred to me that my cognitive thought process was simply projection with no inner substance. I was in dreamland, totally unconscious about my actions.

SO JUNG

While studying theater at the Berkeley, I was lucky enough to encounter Carl Jung's work and became a devoted reader of his analytical theories. Jung is not an easy read. The depth of Jung's material is vast and fascinating. His major influence was the exploration of mythology, ancient primordial/historical archetypes, and dream analysis as ways to understand man's collective unconscious, that reservoir of experiences of the human species common to everyone.

Another way of saying this is that the unconscious directs the *self* through the medium of archetypes, myths, dreams, and intuition, thereby provoking the psyche toward self-actualization. The unconscious has a more profound sense of self's ideal than the ego or conscious self. Simply put, the unconscious allows us to make mistakes so that we can go about our business of individuating with the hope of achieving some form of self-mastery.

It occurred to me I had no self-mastery as witnessed by my behavior at my son's wedding. Sure, I had discipline, but I obviously had no mastery over emotions that resided in my unconscious. Since my emotions were hidden, they surfaced in the form of *projection*, the Freudian and Jungian psychological aspect that concerns the unconscious act of denial of a person's own thoughts and emotions, which are then ascribed or projected to the outside world. In my case, I was angry, and that anger was directed against my ex-husband and son; and I didn't know why because I wasn't in touch with my unconscious feelings. Had I understood why I felt the way I felt at the wedding, I could have controlled my outburst and distanced myself from the negative feelings toward me exhibited by my ex-husband and son.

STOP THE WORLD, I WANT TO GET OFF

I made an appointment with Mike, my therapist. It was an "Oh my God" moment. I am only six days older than Mike. We are both Scorpios. He sports a beard and his eyes twinkled behind bushy eyebrows. He is brilliant and funny and is full of stillness, restraint, and wisdom. Mike is not a cognitive therapist; he does not suggest behavioral changes. He does not give advice or tell his clients how to behave. Because he is a Jungian and not a Freudian, he limits the exposure of a client's past history and does not deal with psychological complexes. He considers the past as anecdotal, the present as real, and the unconscious as revelatory. Mike explores the unconscious through a person's dreams as the primary means of cultivating mindful awareness of self and developing healthy interpersonal relationships with others.

Mike also made me more aware of how projection, one of many human defense mechanisms, caused harm to others as well as to myself. If I am projecting, I am in denial; if I am in denial, my conscious mind doesn't have to deal with my suppressed feelings. This was a key to my wedding bell blues. This was a start to healing.

My rant to Mike: I was beside myself to think that I had single-handedly ruined my son's wedding and angry that my new daughter-in-law thought I was the biggest bitch on the planet and the most selfish woman she had ever met. She had expressed this volatile sentiment in a very loud voice in front of my mother, my family, and other strangers gathered for breakfast at the restaurant the morning after the wedding. She wanted to know why I was at the restaurant.

"You have no right being here. You left the wedding. You should leave now," she burst out at me.

"I'm staying," I said with hostility. "I'm not going anywhere."

"Well, you should go," she loudly proclaimed.

I stood my ground but felt the guillotine was next on her list. Did she just say, "Off with her head"?

The new groom came over to rescue the situation.

INT. RESTAURANT - MORNING
The restaurant is crowded with a wedding party. AARON and JOAN are huddled in a corner away from the booths.

                    AARON
    We acknowledged you. What does
    it matter that it was at the end?

                    JOAN
Why didn't I get to say something?

                    AARON
It wasn't part of the plan.

                    JOAN
I should have spoken at the
wedding. I asked you earlier ...

                    AARON
And I said no. You didn't do much
of anything as far as wedding
plans. We asked you to come to
the food tasting, and you couldn't.
You're always busy.

                    JOAN
That's a low blow and not true.
I have a work schedule. You two
wanted the wedding to be yours
without interference.

                    AARON
Besides, we decided you shouldn't
speak because you always make
it about yourself.

The dialogue was getting heated. Everyone witnessed the telenovela playing out in real time. Too bad it wasn't in Spanish so no one could understand. Jonathan came over and abruptly ended the conversation, but not before he took a swipe at me with his pitch-perfect parenting skills.

INT. RESTAURANT - MORNING
JONATHAN walks up to his mother, JOAN.

>JONATHAN
>Mom, you shouldn't have left the room no matter how you felt. You were wrong.

>JOAN
>I was being treated unfairly. And I didn't appreciate your father's attempt at humor at my expense.

>JONATHAN
>He was just kidding. You know Dad.

>JOAN
>Not funny. Twenty minutes of a self-important speech.

>JONATHAN
>But don't you think you were wrong?

>JOAN
>Why do I have to be wrong?

>JONATHAN
>Because you walked out, Mom.

My boyfriend started to say something, and I yanked him away before any more damage could be done. The gods were not happy with me. And to prove it, I discovered that the convertible top on my Volvo was slashed during the night. I was on a roll.

WEDDING BELL BLUES

I told Mike my head was swimming for days, even weeks. I vacillated between anger and defiance tinged with righteousness. I knew I didn't ruin the wedding. The wedding went off without a hitch, and it was beautiful. But why did I leave? My inner child had misbehaved.

My ego ranted on: I felt isolated. I felt marginalized. I felt like my son and new daughter-in-law had purposely imposed a "stop Mom" alert during the wedding. I couldn't figure out why it was such a big deal that I not speak.

Mike stared at me as if I was from another planet.

"Do you actually think that you somehow were the cause of your son's unhappiness and the cause of your daughter-in-law's rage?" he asked quietly, peering at me with an intensity that made me bolt upright.

I was startled by the question. Did Mike mean I had a choice about how I felt? That I could actually not blame myself for being disrespectful and narcissistic? What a concept! I was off and running. I was ready to dive in and begin to find some things out about myself. It was time to ask a boatload of questions.

But I wasn't even close to asking the crucial questions because I was so tied up with those moments in the past that continued to hurt me and so blasted unconscious about what transpired at the wedding and the emotions attached to my family and to my ex-husband. I did not possess the insight to be fully aware of what was going on inside of me, let alone understand the dynamic of the event.

I recalled what Eckhart Tolle wrote in *The Power of Now,* "Don't get trapped inside events and situations ... dis-identify."

Easy for Eckhart to say. It wasn't his son's wedding.

"Write down your dreams," Mike instructed. "You've been unconscious about your relationship with your family, with yourself, and especially with your ex-husband. You're subjecting yourself to past emotions and bringing them forward. This wedding business has nothing to do with you. Your son and daughter-in-law were projecting."

Of course, it had something to do with me. I was a participant, a player in the play within the play. But something new was going on inside of me. Maybe my inner demons were working their way into consciousness, but the outer forces were waging battle against my inner self. This journey felt interminable.

Incredibly, there seemed to be a way out. Dreams. But dreams seem illogical and confusing at first. In therapy, I learned that my dreams told me what I was unconsciously suppressing—those emotions, feelings, resolves, struggles, and conflicts that were buried deep in my psyche. I quickly latched on to the idea that bringing this information into my consciousness was truly valuable for my personal growth.

People say they don't remember dreams or that they don't dream at all, but everyone dreams many times during the night. I desperately wanted to remember my dreams, so before I came to full consciousness in the morning, I would recall my dreams; then I would write them in my computer journal and take them to Mike.

Mike cautioned me not to interpret my dreams. This kind of inner work must be done with a trained Jungian therapist. An important point to remember, however, is that the people in dreams are not actually real people. Every person in a dream is an aspect of self, and these selves help identify the emotions and feelings that are trapped inside the psyche. Denial only increases the possibility that the inner demons that stay stuck in the psyche will manifest themselves as projections onto innocent people we love.

My therapist's interpretation of my dreams helped me stop the insanity of my personal struggle—freeing me of my guilt, fear, shame, and, finally, denial. As my emotional responses became more conscious, the negative impact on others lessened. I was creating a framework for being present.

During my therapy sessions, there was a reoccurring theme that developed. It had to do with blame. Because I was not in touch with my psyche, I felt that I was the sole reason for things going wrong in my relationships or with parent-child situations. If I could only turn the bad into good, then everything would be better.

One day, in session, I told Mike that I had a dream about driving a Volkswagen van filled with people.

"You are not responsible for all those people in your van," Mike said. "Try driving a car instead or ride a bike and then see if you can walk alone."

I switched to a bike in my dreams and occasionally walked alone. I became less the nurturer and worked to develop more awareness regarding my family members; then I mixed insight with some healthy detachment. I became less reactive and more in control of my emotions, and communication improved.

RIDE A PAINTED PONY

Liberation was at hand. The Catholic girl's ingrained low self-esteem was about to end. Why was I so worried when other people said that I was too intense, too passionate, too smart, when my sons criticized me or projected on me, when men ran away from me or ran up to me because they can spot a nurturer a mile away? I always used to say that if I'm sitting in a bar, the alcoholic would slither up next to me, and I'd be the next sucker in his life. Even though I refer to myself as a bottom line girl with very little nuances, I'm as vulnerable inside as anyone else. I go unconscious as fast as anyone, and "stuff happens."

My friend Peter tells me that I'm really a woman of the 1950s. He is only partially right. I'm part old-fashioned girl and part Mother Earth on speed. I can either put people off with my directness or attract overly dependent people who won't let me go.

"You're just being who you are, an unapologetic bundle of energy," Mike said. "And by the way, there's nothing wrong with you. Just keep dreaming, and you'll find out more about yourself."

"Nothing wrong with me? Really? There's always something wrong with me," I responded to Mike with self-deprecating humor.

"Just keep exploring the mystery of life, of love; move through it with joy and without expectation," Mike soulfully chanted as if it were his mantra. "Embrace your intensity, your energy, and your fantasies." Then he said cautiously, "You still need to tame your inner pony."

"What's my inner pony?" I asked with the voice of an eight-year-old.

"Sit with your emotions for as long as it takes," Mike said to me. "When things don't feel right, when you feel sad or angry, be with the emotion, stay with it, embrace it. The emotion will resolve itself, and you will feel better."

Self-restraint is an empowering concept truly worthy of exploration. And that kind of self-mastery purported to be an absolutely agonizing challenge.

I never met a man like Mike. I've sent other people to him, and we are all madly in love with Mike the therapist and yes, of course, the man too, because no woman has ever met Mike's identical twin in real life. I'd like to seriously consider cloning him.

Working with Mike over a year's time brought me some revelations. He pointed out that I did not need to do anything for a time regarding my sons.

"Stay away from your family, from discussions about the wedding," Mike advocated. "Let them come to you."

This was a huge challenge for me. The therapeutic process was beginning to feel like being in recovery. But I persevered. Healing had to begin somewhere.

There were forays of communication. Every once in a while, Jonathan and Carli ran reconnaissance to assess the situation. Several months passed. There were flurries of e-mails, and then nothing.

It was November and my birthday month. Aaron called, and we met at Starbucks in Venice. I was nervous. So was he. The conversation didn't go well, but we both hung in. We agreed to talk again. We parted without resolution. He said he wouldn't forgive me.

I don't know if I have ever been forgiven, but in time, life with my sons returned to some normalcy. For a long time, nothing was said; and I continued to watch the dogs, house-sit, and be available with love. Small intentions.

I don't have the luxury of going to therapy now, but I still do the inner work with meditation and dreams as my primary tools. I try to practice restraint, although Corinne says my "inner pony" still needs to be reined in. Mike also refers to the illusive it as "the little girl inside of me."

"Don't completely get rid of her," he proffered. "She's what makes you who you are."

EPILOGUE: WATCH OUT FOR THAT CURVEBALL

Sometime ago, my son Aaron, Alyse and their baby, Greyson, watched their belongings vanish inside a moving van outside their home in Venice. Without fanfare, they got in their car and drove to Las Vegas to live and work.

I knew about the inevitability of this move for months. Their actual departure did not make my pain any easier. I have no family left in Los Angeles, but I do have enough plane tickets to Las Vegas to last me through the end of the year.

Text message from Alyse to Gran
Can u babsit at 12
got yoga class
got time or
does Carli have u booked?
let me knw

CHAPTER 5
DON'T CALL ME GRANDMA!

I never thought much about my sons' reproductive activities. If I had given birth to a girl, I might have been more interested. Females have the same plumbing; and we relate on the level of PMS, urinary tract infections, bladder infections, yeast infections, birth control, vaginal versus C-section births, lumps in the breast, belly fat, menopause, hormone-replacement therapy versus homeopathic therapy, hot flashes, and night sweats. What else is there? Oh yes, we all fall madly in love.

But I produced boys, and the closest we ever came to talking about sex concerned the use of condoms. When Jonathan was in the eighth grade, I took him to a drugstore in Beverly Hills and bought him a box of condoms. "Don't forget to use them," I prompted when we got home. I have no idea what he did with them, but I knew he was not a virgin, hence the box of condoms. I knew that because he told me he got laid in the seventh grade while living with his father in Las Vegas during his bar mitzvah year. He also was introduced to porno films, pot, and poker. I guess there were no boundaries that year. Prior to that, when Jonathan was in the fifth grade, he asked me about blow jobs, as in, "Did you give Dad blow jobs?" I was utterly speechless as I continued to fold clothes from the dryer. I told him we'd talk about it later, much later when he was about sixteen. By that age, he would have gotten his own blow job(s), and we would need no further discourse on the subject.

Aaron must have learned about sex from his brother or some random friend or David. The only curiosity he had about sex (that I know of) was as a high school junior when he asked David why he stayed with me. David's classic reply was, "Because she's a great lay." Good old David. The man didn't mince words. When he was a junior in high school, Aaron told me he had sex with his girlfriend.

"Don't forget to use protection," I said with firmness. "And I'm taking you to my AIDS education class next Wednesday."

I was an AIDS educator at the time and insisted that Aaron learn about this new sexually transmitted disease.

"Okay, Mom," he said pleasantly. "But I'm not at risk."

"Everyone's at risk, Aaron," I replied sternly. "Even senior citizens. Take it seriously."

I went out and bought him a box of condoms.

I never inquired again about my sons' sexual activities unless they volunteered information. There were brief conversations from time to time, but my boys made their own decisions in that area. They were fully informed. I presume I would have been more forthcoming with daughters talking about sexual matters. Women talk about female sex issues frequently. It is one of the ways in which we relate to each other. Sex and Hollywood gossip are also favorite topics.

CALL ME GRAN

In all my years, I had never remotely entertained the possibility of becoming a grandmother. In fact, the idea of being a grandmother did not particularly interest me. It brands a woman as an "old broad." When my date asks, "Who are the kids in the pictures on your bookcase?"

I stutter, "Uh ... uh ... those are my grandsons."

To which my date replies, with underwhelming politeness, "You're a grandmother? Wow."

My mother was not particularly nurturing as a grandmother. Her grandsons came over for lunch every once in a while; they played a little, and then we went home. No overnights. No elaborate vacations to Disneyland. With the exception of holiday meals, the connection was not effusive.

My father, Papa John, was another story. The boys adored him. He knew how to relate to them, to be funny, to tease and joke, and to show affection. As they grew older, he was living most of the time in various states of an alcoholic fog. They knew about his drinking, so as kids will do, they enjoyed the good times. They did not judge Papa John because they had grown up with him and loved him.

And so, when it came time that I was going to become a grandmother, I had no idea what to do, what to expect, or how to conduct myself. I just knew I wasn't going to be called Grandma. I kept replaying in my mind the scene from Terms of Endearment where Shirley MacLaine sat at the head of the table having dinner with her family, and her granddaughter called her Grandma.

"Don't call me Grandma!" Shirley brayed. "How many times do I have to tell you that?"

I was driving to Las Vegas the morning that Carli's water broke, hoping I would get there in time for the baby's birth and trying to think of a fun name befitting a grandmother. Noah Wylie's character in the TV series ER called his grandmother Gan. Young children have a difficult time pronouncing r's, so Gran came out Gan. I decided to put the r back in the word, and all grandchildren would henceforth call me Gran.

Jordan Mac was born on February 12, 2005, in Las Vegas, Nevada. It was the most joyous moment in my life since the birth of my two boys. I was unexpectedly amazed by my emotion. The idea was inspirational; the reality was indescribable. I paced the hospital corridors with joy and made phone calls indiscriminately. I loved this baby immediately. It was a miracle and a mystery all wrapped up in a beautiful bundle.

The immediate family, including my mother, the first-time great-grandmother, was elated. Even my ex-husband showed signs of emotion. And Jonathan, the new father, was changed by his new status. Family love and responsibility can have enormous positive effects on a person's psyche. There was instant gratification all around at the birth of this first grandchild.

WHO'S ON FIRST?

After Jordan was born, my next mission was, how am I going to bond with this baby? How will this baby love me? I already loved Jordan. But how will Jordan know me and grow to love me?

I set about a task for myself to make a conscious effort to be a dedicated and supportive grandmother. I suspect this need was born of ego and the desire to be loved by my grandchildren. I wasn't sufficiently conscious to understand that love is created organically with a child, or maybe I had just forgotten. The important role was simply to be present and loving. However, when Jordan was born, I had no desire to share this baby with anyone but his parents.

I had to learn to be a grandmother the hard way, and it was a rocky road at the beginning. I drove or flew to Las Vegas once a month and tried to hold on to my Gran territory. I was attentive, always available, helpful, loving and devoted. When I heard that the other grandparents (whom I adore) were going to visit, the hair stood up on the back of my neck. I was single, and they were a couple, a grandparent couple! My ex wasn't helpful. He didn't identify as being the other half of our fake togetherness as a grandparenting team, so Jordan didn't understand the idea that both of us together were his grandparents on his father's side. I am not sure when that might happen; maybe I'd have to wait until his bar mitzvah.

Then I brought around the Sicilian, and that ended in disaster because he became stupidly possessive of Jordan and interfered with my being Gran. I just wanted him to get the hell out of the room most of the time, and I had to—blast it all—admonish him not to create distractions. Men can be really annoying when it comes to playing with little children. They make the kid crazy, and then Gran has to settle the little guy down and feed him and focus him; and all the while, the grown-up guy is making ridiculous faces at the kid to make him laugh while he is eating because it's all about the grown-up wanting the attention from the kid.

The situation got complicated with my wanting to break up with the Sicilian, Jonathan not wanting the Sicilian around anymore, and the Sicilian not wanting to extricate himself from the picture. Lesson learned: Think long and hard about bringing a nonfamily member into the family unit unless there is duct tape nearby. The situation doesn't bring out the best in anyone.

I guess it's possible to introduce an unknown element into a family, but it has the potential to produce conflicting emotions and family possessiveness. My sons are not overtly interested when I mention a potential boyfriend. I'm sure it is a question of trust and how well the man treats me. It is only natural that my sons want their mother to be respected, to be honestly loved and cherished by a man. That's how they interact with their wives. I knew my sons were a tough act to put up with for any suitor, but if a man upsets the family dynamic, he will not be warmly embraced.

WHO'S ON SECOND?

I did my fair share of driving Jonathan nuts in the first six to eight months of Jordan's life. But it wasn't so for Carli, my daughter-in-law, who is one cool cookie. She has never admonished me for anything I have done as a gran. She loved that I got up in the morning early to give a morning bottle or feed the boys or take them out to Starbucks to get everyone coffee. Carli was able to relax, sleep in, and generally felt a sense of comfort while I was visiting.

However, Jonathan has had plenty to say when I overstepped my boundaries. And I was not always sure where the boundary lines were drawn. Conflicts quickly flared up. Women who have raised their own children have their own set of priorities when it comes to raising children. There are many books on grandparenting, but most of them don't translate into actual reality.

"We are more relaxed with our kids," Jonathan warned me. "Don't push your style on us."

"But look how you and Aaron turned out," I would counter.

"Mom, don't interfere," he responded like a drill sergeant.

I spent some time wondering what kind of inappropriate behavior I exhibited during the first year of Jordan's life. Being a grandparent often didn't feel natural, and it was sometimes stressful.

INT. JONATHAN'S KITCHEN - MORNING
JONATHAN is making banana pancakes. JORDAN is running around the family room.

                GRAN
Come on, Jordan, let's get ready for breakfast.

GRAN runs after Jordan. He eludes her. She tries to catch him. He escapes her.

              GRAN (CONT'D)
Jordan, it's time to eat. Settle down.

              JONATHAN
Let him play. He'll come to the table.
Gran retreats. Jordan is hauling his pirate ship into the center of the room.

              GRAN
Jordan, it's time to eat not play.

              JORDAN
No! I wanna watch TV.

              JONATHAN
Leave him alone, Mom. He'll come to the table when the food is ready. He knows what to do.

Jordan ignores Gran.

              JORDAN
I wanna watch Elmo.

              GRAN
He isn't listening.

            JONATHAN
He listens.

              GRAN
No, he doesn't.

            JONATHAN
Back off, Mom. He's not your kid. Jordan, come to the table.

Jordan ignores his father. Jonathan picks up Jordan and takes him to the table. Jordan whines and throws his plate down. Pancakes tumble to the floor.

            JONATHAN
Just stay out of it, Mom. You're causing trouble. I don't like it when you interfere.

This scene continued. I noticed there was no fruit on Jordan's plate. I got some strawberries out of the refrigerator and put them on his plate. Jordan shoved a few in his mouth and started to play with a toy truck, which he had surreptitiously hidden in his hand. He ignored his breakfast, and I tried to encourage him to eat.

INT. JONATHAN'S KITCHEN - MORNING

          JONATHAN

Don't feed him, Mom. He can eat by himself.

Jordan continues to play with his truck. Jonathan sits down at the table.

          JONATHAN

Eat your breakfast, Jordan.

          JORDAN

I don't want to eat.

          GRAN

You have to eat something. You need strong bones to grow.

Gran picks up Jordan's fork.

          JONATHAN

Mom, I told you. Let him do it.

Gran puts the fork down. Jordan picks up the fork, spears a piece of pancake, and flips it up in the air. The dog eats it before it hits the floor.

          GRAN

Put the truck down, Jordan.

JONATHAN
Look, Mom. Jordan isn't your kid. You're crossing boundaries.

I confess that I dislike the word "boundaries." It connotes space issues, limits, borders and restrictions. There is an entire universe of "no" connected to the "boundary" word. Pick up a fork to encourage eating, and you've crossed boundaries. Tell the kids to eat their pancakes, and you are parenting. Ask your grandson to pick up his toys, and you're interfering. There came a point where I felt helpless. It took everything I had inside myself to control my parental impulses and just plain shut up. I'm not very good at it.

I remembered the first time I was changing Jordan's diapers, and my son came in and took over the diapering. "I'll do that, Mom." I stood back and watched, not uttering a word. It was his son after all.

Just recently, I lost it again at IHOP. Drawing with crayons on a Formica table was more than I could handle. I took a time-out instead of responding and risk more parenting from my son.

There are cultures that traditionally encourage the grandchildren to be raised by the grandparents. In some enclaves in the United States, it is expected and even anticipated that grandparents will participate in child rearing. I always loved having my Grandma Rose around, and although she did not participate in my upbringing, I found her presence soothing. Perhaps that is all that is asked of me, but I was too new at the game to realize that I was supposed to express myself only when asked to participate.

Before Luc, my second grandson, was born, I had been subtly lobbying for some focus on toilet training Jordan. When I was raising children, they were potty trained around two. A child couldn't attend preschool wearing a diaper. Of course, this was my issue and not the issue of Jordan's parents. Their chosen preschool accepted children wearing diapers. My surprise was obvious.

So everyone was mad at me, accusing me of pushing the potty issue too hard. But I knew that Jordan knew that he could be potty trained. Resolve was all that was needed. I stayed at the house to babysit for a long weekend during the summer and focused on the potty-training program. We got somewhere, but his parents were still unconcerned, and it was not reinforced when they returned. Boy, did I cross those boundaries. And yes, Jordan was potty trained when he started his second year of preschool when the teachers were training all the children in class, and Jordan got it perfectly right with all the other kids who were lining up for the bathroom. It just goes to show you how I don't know nothin' about nothin'.

Upon reflection, I should have stayed out of the family dynamic. However, I didn't live in the Dark Ages. I was an informed parent in the 1970s, and I read books and periodicals and talked with other mothers; and yes, we were a stricter group of parents. My bible was Dr. Haim Ginott's *Between Parent and Child,* a book that revolutionized child-parent communication. Ginott believed that children are like sponges; they are so very impressionable that whatever you put to them makes an impression.

We were Dr. Spock's babies too. I reflected my mother's strict child rearing Spock techniques in some ways, although I believed I had a stronger emotional connection to my sons. Nevertheless, I wanted to keep the peace in my son's household, so the most effective technique was to detach from my opinions. My belief system was not more important than the parents' way of raising children. But the ego mind is a nasty thing to control. I've got to let it all go even though Luc is ready to be potty trained.

By the time my second grandson was born, I had grown into the job and lost my jealousies and the need for territorial imperative, giving it up to my higher power or just ignored the comments. The truth is that being a grandparent is different from being a parent. I'm still learning, and I hope I'm mellowing as the overall feelings of joy and gratitude grow each time I see them.

Jonathan and Carli implement many creative ideas in their children's lives. And Aaron and Alyse follow suit. I love the idea of early music listening, music classes, Mommy and Me classes, early swimming lessons, and soccer or T-ball activities. I always go to their games and practices when I am in Las Vegas. My grandsons love all music, know lyrics from their fathers' favorite rock tunes, and dance to the beat of any song. Books are introduced within the first year.

I read to the boys and go on field trips to Barnes & Noble. Jordan has already told me that he wants to be an anthropologist and study dinosaurs. He also wants to be an astronaut and a ski instructor. I credit his parents for his unending curiosity.

Yet, Gran isn't all about books and music and getting in the pool for swimming lessons. Gran is about having fun and introducing her grandsons to unique experiences. My favorite outing with Luc was the summer day I spent alone with him at the beach on Balboa Island. We were at the swings and slides on the beach, and before I knew it, Luc was surrounded by a group of young children. It was a delight to watch him interact at one and a half years of age. It was getting close to margarita time and dinner, so I took him to a Mexican cantina/sports bar nearby. Luc watched baseball, rocked out to music, and high-fived the guys. He ate and drank like a champ (lemonade, of course) and was so happy he didn't want to leave. Luc was one of the best dates I've ever had.

LIKE MOTHER, LIKE DAUGHTER

There is an axiom that goes, "The older we get, the less patience we have with young children." My mother had very little patience throughout her life, and I consciously reflected to myself that I would always try to have patience with my children and their progeny. In particular, I didn't like my mother's lack of tolerance and shortness with me. She was more concerned with order than with nurturing. When Jordan visited my mother, she was always on edge about what he would pick up and how he would disrupt her things. She did not understand that he was using his imagination to play. I rarely brought Luc to her home.

Sometimes I get spooked because I can feel my mother channeling through me. I hear it in my voice and view it in my manner, and I shudder—grant me the serenity to know the difference. I must be mindful of the order of generations and the dynamics of their interrelatedness.

There were many aspects of my upbringing that were positive, and I am thankful to my mother for being a role model. She had a wonderful skill set, which included discipline, order, and time management. She was a creative woman: a compulsive seamstress, a businesswoman who owned a construction company with my father, and the designer of all the homes and apartment complexes they built.

In her so-called old age, at about seventy-five, she turned to teaching senior aerobics. Her crowning moment of glory came when she was voted Miss Senior Citizen of Las Vegas. She finally retired from teaching after making a senior aerobics video in her eighties. Then she took up tap dancing with a vengeance.

I will always be respectful of the ideals my mother taught me, of the values she instilled in me, and of her tenaciously positive attitude toward life. I hope I can pass these attitudes and values onto my grandchildren in time.

UNDER ONE ROOF

It is important for generations to communicate effectively because there may be a possibility that grandma and grandpa will live together under the same roof with their offspring. Statistics show that living with one's adult children and grandchildren is becoming increasingly popular as the number of households containing multiple generations rises and the cost of long term health care increases yearly. Those of us in our sixties are living longer; and the thought that keeps running through my mind isn't "How great that will be," but "I'm going to outlive my retirement savings and depend on the kindness of my sons." The other thought is, "I don't want to live in a state of longevity that requires me to spend my last days on earth in dementia, helpless, and a burden to my family." I hope that we are given the choice to die when we want and with dignity. At least, that is what I told my sons.

Further complicating generational issues is a host of economic challenges now facing boomers—the stock market's erratic performance, job losses, early retirement, and a host of bad governmental and business decisions—could gradually result in a major rearrangement of family life in America, which might include adult children and their families moving in with parents, either for the short or long term. Other common reasons for boomers living with their children might be the loss of a spouse, particular health care needs, inability to sustain home costs, and the wiping out of retirement and pension plans.

I just got word from my son, Jonathan that I should not worry about my vanishing assets. "You've got your sons, Mom," he assured me. Maybe I do, and maybe I don't. Gran expects the unexpected.

The best-case multigenerational scenario can occur when a family embraces the demographic differences in a household. The ideal would be to provide sufficient physical space as well as economic advantages in an atmosphere of unconditional love. It would require flexibility, not having to always be right, and no outsized egos. The behavior code would require personal respect, kindness, and courtesy. These are tall orders for us humans. Yet, the outcome might result in a heart-opening way of life that is more familycentric in tone and style. Yet, in my situation, I know I would find it unbelievably challenging living under one roof with either of my boys.

Nevertheless, I hope I'm not going to be put out to pasture in some retirement community unless I am the one who suggests that alternative. I don't play cards or do crossword puzzles. However, I might want to learn bridge to keep my mind active. And I probably could get a head of steam up to tap-dance with the senior ladies so I could wear all those garish Las Vegas costumes. My mother looked great in them! My sons tease me that I will end up teaching senior tango and gentle senior yoga. They keep forgetting that I'm already a senior.

Grandparenting is a true challenge and another journey to encounter. I am still amazed at how much love it involves, how much mindfulness it encompasses, and how much joy it gives to my life. Last weekend, I put together a dinosaur puzzle with Jordan. I think I had more fun than he did.

I guess you could call me Grandma if you want. Even Shirley MacLaine succumbed and embraced the chance to love her progeny unconditionally.

PART 2
SEX

Text message from Dr. Demento
Can't go forward
don't love u enough
fell out of love with u
& fell in love w/ my house

CHAPTER 6
MEN AND OTHER SOCIOPATHS
I HAVE KNOWN

I have always been concerned that I don't know much about men, and I certainly don't have a great track record over the years with my relationships. The truth is I can't understand how men think, how their emotional psyche works, and how and why they make decisions about love. I am usually an optimist; but even years from now, even if I do find that one man/needle in the haystack that I might fall madly in love with again and who complements my natural exuberance for life, I will still know nothing about men.

I don't think I had a very successful relationship with my ex-husband: there were two strong egos, two different agendas. We had some common values, but my ex was missing the most important value of family first. Then there was David, my significant other, and we had an unconventional, outside-the-box relationship. Although David was a man like no other I have ever met or ever loved, sadly, in the end, I didn't know as much about the man as I had thought.

On the first day of my producing class at the American Film Institute, David sealed my heart. He went around the table and asked each of us to give a brief statement about why we wanted to learn how to produce films. When I remarked that I had come from the theater world, David interrupted me with authority and a large dose of irony.

INT. CLASSROOM, AFI - MORNING
JOAN and film students sit around a table.
DAVID stands at the front of the room near a blackboard.

          DAVID
    (with a twinkle in his eyes)
Theater is dead, Joan.

          JOAN
What do you mean by that, David?

          DAVID
Plays are like stained glass windows hung in medieval churches for the purpose of teaching the masses about Christian mythology.

          JOAN
So we aren't learning anything from plays?

          DAVID
Today film is the best way to express philosophical ideas and modern social thought. We don't learn from stained glass anymore, and we don't learn much from plays either.

          JOAN
But that's exactly why I'm in film school, David.

DAVID
Good. Just so long as we are on
the same page.

David was out in the stratosphere with his opinions, but it happened that his remark about theater was intuitive and dead-on, and I had been thinking the same thing for the last two years. I was hooked, intrigued, and in love.

And David was everywhere around me with his knowledge and sparkling wit. A month into the first semester, I was standing in the aisle, hovered over a desk as he walked behind me. "Nice ass," he whispered and kept walking. I wasn't surprised or offended. We both knew something unspoken was going on, and it was not just a flirtation.

A drink and then another drink. A dinner and a kiss. Stories exchanged. We both went to Berkeley in the sixties; and that, along with adoring Sinatra, is enough to bond any two people together. The conversations were always intellectually stimulating and tremendously fun. David was truly authentic, a man for all seasons.

One night, after class, he asked me to dinner. I told him I couldn't because my boys were at home.

"If they are home now, they are old enough to make themselves a sandwich for dinner," he flatly remarked. "Call and tell them you'll be home after dinner."

That night, David asked me to marry him.

I figured when two people connect so strongly, some star or planetary alignment in the universe or some force of nature had to be pushing us together. Three months later, he moved in to my rented house, but not before I had to move another man out. I'm impulsive, I know, but David was unique.

I never thought about how it was going to be to live with David. We had the same intellectual sensibility, an uncanny sense of irony and compatible humor, and the creativity to improvise our lives and our love. He was an adventurer, an artist (he studied to be a sculptor before being recruited by the CIA), and a football fanatic who looked at the game as a finely tuned war plan or a special ops assignment that was a matter life or death. He was so easy to live with that for the first several months, I felt like I should wait for the other shoe to drop. It never did, but we never did get married.

During the last few months of my first year at AFI, I wrote my first screenplay at David's suggestion. He told me to write about what I knew, and I knew about Las Vegas when the mob ran the town because my ex-husband and his partner were lawyers for the mob.

"Write the script with an actress in mind for the role," David directed.

It was agonizing and frustrating and empowering all at the same time, but I wrote the screenplay for Cher. I almost got it made with Paramount, and I was on a roll. We wrote the second screenplay together; and the experience was joyous, creative, bawdy, and ethereal. We wrote more scripts and took hundreds of meetings pitching and slogging through the unfathomable and illusive business called entertainment. It was yin and yang all the way, and it was truly joyful because I did it with David.

We stayed together for almost eight years after Aaron left for college, the last six of which offered numerous economic and domestic compromises. And David kept secrets and told half-truths, and that made our last years together a struggle. Finally, we just stopped communicating. It never occurred to me that perhaps David was an invention of his own making. Or he was an invention of my own mind.

When we parted, there was a profound sense of loss. David will always be the Renaissance man, the bon vivant, the fearless warrior, and the dedicated stepfather who never hesitated to take a leap of faith for me and whose love I will always cherish. He was "the man."

A HARD ACT TO FOLLOW

Enter the rebound. Why do we always fall for the clichés? It's utterly damnable! Can't we be more original? Can't we just wait for a respectable time to mourn our loss? Do we have to immediately jump from one man or woman to another to fill the illusionary big void in our lives? Can't we enjoy ourselves and not be compelled to embrace the neuroses of some other man or woman? Aren't we enough for ourselves? Do we have to rely on others to meet all our emotional and psychological needs? I was fifty-nine when the rebound showed up. I did not take time to rest, to forgive, or to still my mind and body. It just proves that at any age, we know nothing. This was truly an unconscious moment for me.

In the fifteen or so years I have been dancing tango, I was never involved romantically with another tango dancer (Buenos Aires doesn't count because it's not in the United States) and never had a boyfriend in my tango community. I wanted to dance tango and not to pick up men. I don't give male tango dancers a second thought beyond how they understand the music and how they gracefully lead a woman on the floor. The tango world is a seemingly conducive environment to fall in love; but if a dancer is vulnerable, sad, and needy, it portends nothing but heartbreak. I had all of those feelings going on inside of me when I went to a tango event in Las Vegas just as I was breaking up with David.

I met Dr. Demento (code name) years before at a tango festival in the Midwest. I was standing on the side of the dance floor during a tango break when a fast rock-and-roll tune began to play. Dr. Demento pulled me onto the dance floor, and we bolted into action. I was in terrible aerobics shape and barely held on to the finish. We walked off the floor to the sound of applause. Demento saw that I was almost in respiratory failure, so he laid me down on a table and got close to my face.

"Do you need mouth to mouth?" he whispered in his best bedside manner. "No, I'm fine," I gasped.

My heart was pounding so fast I thought I was going to pass out.

I'm a sucker for romantic gestures. Then I unconsciously make an idiotic leap from the gesture to falling in love. It's impossible to resist a moment of gallantry—like a man asking you if you'd like a foot massage after a private tango lesson, like a man putting you in his car and kissing you just before he closes the door, like twirling a woman around on a Parisian street corner at three in the morning and kissing her passionately, or like asking a woman to get on a plane and fly first-class to Boston for Thanksgiving weekend on Nantucket.

When consciousness finally returns after the romantic gesture passes, I might be able to recognize the superficiality of the moment—that such a gesture possesses no spiritual depth, no connection to reality, and, more often than not, leads to something resembling a contact sport. I've encountered exceptions, however, as in the Boston man who asked me to marry him on the banks of Lake Pontchartrain in the city of New Orleans.

True to Demento's nature, it was all romantic gesture. He was perfectly charming and did all the right things at the beginning. It was nice to still be in the dating game, and being older and vulnerable made it even more intense. Demento and I lived in different cities, so it was fun to travel one weekend to his city as he returned to Los Angeles for the off weekends. But his trips to Los Angeles became more frequent, more specific in terms of "Let's go shopping on Melrose" or "I want to see vintage furniture in Venice." I'd spend hours watching him ogle the odd 1950s couch, fondle the 1960s red leather retro chair, study a Japanese kimono, or closely examine a shiny Chinese lacquer plate. Demento was also a clotheshorse and loved Fred Segal's, an upscale boutique in Los Angeles where all the rich and famous shop.

What I noticed particularly was how the art of the purchase was the perfect way to please himself. He probably wanted to be alone on these shopping forays; but he needed a tour guide, a designated driver, and some sex along the way. I discovered over a period of seven months that I was literally the conduit to furnishing his home, which turned out to be his ultimate goal.

But then suddenly, I'd have a catch in my throat or fuzzy feelings in my stomach when he showed up with flowers. These were not just ordinary store-bought flowers, but beautifully, artistically arranged esoteric flowers from exotic flower shops. Demento loved flowers. He even painted them. Every time I saw him, he gave me a unique arrangement, and it would be so romantic. Who wouldn't fall in love with a man who understood his feminine mystique?

My addiction to Demento was that, and—I want to be perfectly candid here—I loved the sex with him. After six years of a dry spell, I rediscovered my sex drive as my hormones kicked into action. I was almost sixty, and the looming question was, will I ever have sex again? I felt as raw and unsubtle as when I first asked the son of a cantor to take my virginity. In retrospect, the sex part was not very healthy because I probably became a sex addict with him. In fact, I'm sure of it because when he finally left me, I felt his presence in and on and around my body for months afterward. And to torture myself, I replayed the tape over and over in my mind while driving my car or falling asleep or standing in line at Whole Foods.

When I saw the film What the Bleep #$*! Do We Know, I understood that under the influences of love and sex my brain chemistry had altered and my body was hormonally paying the price. I was addicted not to drugs, but to the rush I got from the emotional response to my sexual behavior. The response was like being high on cocaine when dopamine and serotonin kick into the body with a vengeance.

What I didn't know was that when Demento left Los Angeles and returned to his own turf, his ardor cooled. This was typical and consistent neurotic behavior provoked by a terror of commitment.

Suddenly, Demento asked me to go to New York City with him and then on to Upstate to visit his mother. Thrilled, I bought the ticket. Okay, he should have bought the ticket, but I was new at dating. I was an untamed pony longing for attention and more sex. And I was going to meet his mother! Then out of the blue, he suddenly called to cancel the trip and to cancel me out of his life.

"I don't love you enough to go forward," he said one night to me on the phone a month before we were to go to New York.

I felt like I was hit with a two-by-four. My brain turned to mush. I'm on the phone, so I couldn't slap him across the face or even get physically violent. The little voice inside me said, "Be graceful. Be a lady; show him you don't give a damn." But my raging anger, my inner pony said, "Hey, this was my vacation! You disgusting, lying son of ..." I was very close to losing my dinner.

INT. JOAN'S LIVING ROOM - NIGHT
JOAN is on the phone, visibly upset. She paces around the room.

                    JOAN
          But I was supposed to meet your
          mother, remember? I bought a
          ticket to New York.

She pulls the phone off her ear and looks to see who is interrupting her call.

                    JOAN
          Just a minute. I've got another
          call.

She presses a button on the phone.

                    JOAN
                (whispering)
          I can't talk, Jonathan. I'm on a
          call.

The following conversation is INTERCUT.

                    JONATHAN
          Why are you whispering? You're
          talking on the phone. You don't
          have to whisper. What's wrong?
          You sound weird.

JOAN
Listen, Jonathan. This isn't a good time to talk.

JONATHAN
Who is it? Who are you talking to?

JOAN
I don't want to tell you.

JONATHAN
Mom ... tell me. What's wrong?

JOAN
I've got to go. Demento is breaking up with me.

JONATHAN
I told you, Mom. I told you he was no good, and you wouldn't listen to me. You never listen to me on these things.

JOAN
Who made you God all of a sudden?

JONATHAN
That's why I didn't have a drink with him at the Four Seasons.

JOAN
Okay, you're psychic. I gotta go.

By god, if there ever was a quintessential child-parenting moment, that was it. And he was right!

In the middle of my romance with Demento, I was also warned about Demento by one of my tango maestros who resided and taught in the same city as Demento. He pulled me aside on a weekend visit.

"Watch out," my maestro said, "he'll break your heart."

And I knew he would, and I knew the woman who hosted the tango gathering in her home was going to be Demento's next victim.

I see it all in reverse perspective. I knew something bad was going to happen, and it played out in my mind in a split second of intuition. That's called the sixth sense, or the sixth chakra, and I paid absolutely no attention to my third eye energy field. It seemed Demento had a torrid affair with a dance teacher in his hometown; she dumped him, breaking his heart, and he was still really angry. It turned out I was his rebound. Those pesky, dirty little secrets everybody keeps from each other can ruin a relationship faster than a speeding bullet.

Three months later, Demento had the chutzpah to show up at a tango event in Los Angeles. He was in my neighborhood and called.

"Meet me at Starbucks, please," he said plaintively. "I need to explain."

I didn't want to talk to him and told him so, but curiosity got the better of me, and I walked the two blocks with trepidation. He was sitting casually on a planter.

"Want to get sushi?" he asked casually.

"Are you kidding me, buddy?" I replied incredulously.

"Look, Joan, I can't help the way I feel," he said in all seriousness. "I fell in love with my house and out of love with you."

What planet did this narcissist live on that he wanted to feed himself while he told me that he was just not that into me?

"I feel like I'm in a Woody Allen movie," I said to him without a trace of irony. "Buzz off and have a good life," I said to him as I hit him way too hard in the arm and walked back up the hill to my apartment.

A committed narcissist cannot muster a shred of empathy or humor. I suspected he used women to make him feel important. He was a serial monogamist who packed a wallop of sinister deceit.

Carl Jung would say he suffered from a mother complex, the inability to stop screwing his anima (his soul, his feminine side) and release it to a woman, finally embracing love. So he liked flowers. Big deal.

I have a habit of making up a man to suit my fantasies, which puts a certain burden of expectation on the man. In this case, I wanted Demento to complete my fantasy of romantic love—Western culture's absurd idea. But the truth is there are thousands of men who are a potential mate for a woman and thousands of women who are a mate for a man. Love is not destiny; it's epidemiology. There is not necessarily one true love for every person on the planet. Although I am convinced that men and women want or need to couple, I know there is no guarantee of finding a mate. There is always some vagueness that goes along with matters of the heart. Honesty is hard to come by. The trick is to get past the shame of rejection, own it, and move on.

CONFESSIONS OF AN INTERNET DATER

I had taken on a new client the previous May before I turned sixty, and we hung out sometimes on weekends. I was perversely fascinated by the way she prowled for men on Internet Web sites. It had been over a year since Demento summarily dumped me, and she wondered when I was going to get off my tuchas and date again. My clientele is primarily women, and I don't come in contact with men. So like a woman on a mission, Annie pumped me up for months and finally sat me down in front of a computer to sign up for Internet dating.

"Who wants to date a sixty-year-old?" I lamented.

"You don't look it, so lie about your age," Annie said. "You're still hot. Don't make this difficult, Joan."

I had no idea how many dating sites there were on the Internet. I think there is a site for every conceivable sexual preference. Given my insecure nature, it was only natural that I wanted to find out if a man would find me remotely attractive or if I was ever going to have sex again. But I wouldn't discount the fact that I was really truly looking for a mate, soul or not.

West Los Angeles is the elephant burial ground for dating men. In Brentwood and Santa Monica, guys run from you if you are over thirty. The thought of auditioning for men made me nauseous. I had been unconsciously prowling for a mate at my local Starbucks for years. I recently switched to Peet's Coffee, where a retired man talked to me every morning. One day, he asked for my card, all the while highlighting in yellow whatever was of interest in the New York Times to send to his brother who lived in New York! Even more recently, I almost—but not quite–got picked up in the waiting room of a Santa Monica hospital while my third grandson was being born. He hovered over me and asked for my card. He was more than interested, I thought. Then nada, nothing! I was a passing flirtation along the birth canal that fizzled before I got to my car. And he was a psychologist! Go figure.

The thought of countless meetings to encounter emotional compatibility, to spark intellectual content, to negotiate political beliefs, to test physical chemistry and "please lie down and let me take your pheromone temperature" was bordering on insanity. It sounded like a horror story: fix me up with agony while you pretend to meet up with flair. It wasn't natural. But the idea of never being in love again and living alone for the rest of my life had no immediate appeal. I hate eating by myself and am not crazy about having sex alone.

I thought I should research Internet interest groups before I signed up for the Internet-dating sites. It seemed a safer way to begin the dating process. Common interests could lead to meeting Mr. Right, I thought. There are interest clubs for everything you can possibly imagine. Some forty-three thousand groups cover 3,500 interests, political and personal. Nearly two thousand exist within a twenty-five-mile radius of Los Angeles. I went on Meetup.com's Web site and got exhausted within the first ten minutes. After looking up writers, hikers, bikers, surfers, wine tasters, my interest was spent. I needed a real date.

"Start by signing up for JDate. That's where you should be seen," Annie said.

"What's the difference between JDate and any other site?" I asked naively. "It's for dating Jews. I thought you were supposed to be smart."

I signed up for JDate for three months. Maybe I could find a nice Jewish guy and become "Sadie, Sadie, married lady" again. I had delusions of grandeur traveling with my lover to Paris.

> AGE RANGE: 55–65
> AGE: 56 (oh, what a lie)
> PHYSICALLY ACTIVE: YES (not a lie)
> INTERESTS: DANCE, READING, MOVIES, TRAVEL
> CHILDREN: TWO ADULT SONS
> RAISED JEWISH (of course)
> OCCUPATION: YOGA INSTRUCTOR, WRITER
> DIVORCED: YES (and it was so long ago)
> PROFILE: SEE PROFILE

I reluctantly lied about my age with complete understanding that I eventually would have to tell the truth, and it might not be pretty.

"Now sign up for more sites if you really want to find a man," Annie persisted. "How about Adult Friend Finders?"

"I don't want to have random sex," I said, taking the high road.

"That's a laugh," Annie retorted. "Any site you go on, men just want to get laid. Don't have any illusions. Technically, what you're doing isn't dating."

I also signed up for eHarmony, thinking I was taking the high road. It was an ordeal. Eleven nightmare pages to fill out, and it took a week. And the rules to contact someone were so annoying. Big, big, big mistake for me on that site. To be fair, eHarmony has improved communications between clients. A few months later,

I concurrently signed up on Yahoo.com for three months and on Match.com for six months in the event neurotic Jews became impossible to deal with. Little did I know that neurotic Jews were also on other sites looking for non-Jewish women.

Before I even put my picture up on JDate (I had written my profile but couldn't figure out how to post a photo because I was technically challenged), I received an email the day I pushed the Submit key. The potential date elaborated on his posted profile and hooked me in with his humor. He wanted to see me the next night and asked for my phone number. Gee wiz, if I had known how easy Internet dating was going to be, I would have stopped my endless protestations.

Before I ever met Ben (code name), I wanted him to be "the one": to be the real man, like David, and not the sociopath, the *puer*, the narcissist, the commitment phobic, the most neurotic Jew I ever met, or whatever mess they always turn into.

EXT. STARBUCKS, SAN VICENTE, NIGHT
BEN and JOAN walk toward each other. Ben takes Joan's arm. There is definite attraction.

>BEN
>We're in a lot of trouble. Let's go for a walk.

>They walk down the street arm in arm without much conversation. At the end of the block, they turn around and walk back to Starbucks.

INT. STARBUCKS, NIGHT
BEN and JOAN enter Starbucks.

>BEN
>What'd ya want?

JOAN
Chai latte and a piece of carrot cake.

BEN
(smiles)
You're a Jewess, aren't you?

JOAN
Yeah, kinda, sort of, but yeah.

BEN
You're going to tell me what that means, right?

JOAN
If I ever get my carrot cake.

They sit at a corner table. Ben watches Joan eat.

JOAN (CONT'D)
Wanna bite?

BEN
Hurry up and finish.

JOAN
Why can't I just enjoy this moment?

Ben leans over and kisses Joan with a mouthful of food.

BEN
That's why.

Ben throws the rest of Joan's
carrot cake in the trash.

      BEN
Let's go.

Ben and Joan casually walk out
of Starbucks.

EXT. STARBUCKS - NIGHT

      JOAN
Where are we going?

      BEN
You'll figure it out.

  I was leading Ben to my apartment in disbelief. Even at sixty, there is no logic to falling in love, or was it just plain lust?
  My apartment had no furniture. I gave everything away weeks before thinking I would redecorate after David left. I have a one-bedroom, so it didn't need much. It was July and hot. I threw a few pillows on the floor, and we lay down next to each other.

INT. JOAN'S APARTMENT - NIGHT

      JOAN
I think this is insane behavior for
two sixty-year-olds.

      BEN
     (defensively)
I'm not sixty yet.

> JOAN
> Then, I'm the older woman. How does it feel?
>
> BEN
> Who better to do this than people who have reached the age of reason?
>
> JOAN
> I don't think I ever reached the age of reason.
>
> Ben kisses Joan passionately again and again. He takes her in his arms and leads her to the bedroom.

I don't think I had known him more than half an hour when we made love like we had been making love all our lives.

Three days later, Ben asked me to marry him.

"Where would we do that?" I asked, trying to be urban cool.

"City hall," he said without missing a beat.

Boy, did I want to do something absolutely crazy and insane and get married to a perfect stranger! I was about to say, "Sure, let's do it"; but I thought my sons would commit me to an institution, and my brother would annul the marriage, but my mother would be so pleased because her daughter was finally married again, and her life would be fulfilled. And my life would change from single to double and be more complicated, but more wonderful.

"Maybe we should give it a little time," I said sweetly. "We've only known each other three days."

We were two Jews with the same rhythm of speech, the same shtick, similar education and interests, both writers who loved our humor and loved everything about each other. The energies were perfectly matched. I saw him for four months, but we only had one date. I took him to see *Hairspray* two weeks after we met because I had free tickets, and we tore the play apart. He asked me not to wear my thong. Boy, was I in love.

The rest of the romance was mostly in my apartment or on his boat. They were Ben's sanctuaries. He only felt safe in those places.

"Why don't we ever go out to dinner?" I asked sometime during the first trimester.

"Everyone does that," Ben asked defensively. "We don't need to do what everyone does. Do you need to do that?"

"Well, Ben, it might be nice to be out in public for a change," I said seriously.

"I take you sailing. What more do you want?"

Several times, we hung out at his sailboat in the marina and sailed or cleaned the boat, made love in the cramped cubbyhole of the hull, ate dinner and played Trivial Pursuit. I kept one secret from him. I get deathly seasick, but I loved to sail. He loved Ralph's fried chicken, Chinese food, Jeopardy! and 60 Minutes. And he loved me for four months.

INT. JOAN'S BEDROOM - MORNING
BEN is getting dressed. JOAN watches him.

                        BEN
          I think you should go out and
          date, baby.

                        JOAN
          You're kidding, right? I'm with
          you. I'm dating you.

                        BEN
          How do you know I'm the one?
          I've had years of dating, even
          been engaged once.

                    JOAN
              (blurts out)
        I don't want to see anyone else.
        We've been together four months.
        Why are you saying this to me?

                    BEN
        That's about as long as I stay
        with a woman.

                    JOAN
        (after a long pause, takes the
                   challenge)
        Sure, I'll date other men.

                    BEN
        Maybe you'll fall in love.

                    JOAN
        I'm in love ... with you, you ass-
        hole.

    The same *puer* issue, the same eternal youth. Get too close to a woman, think you might be falling in love with her, and it's time to go. Typically, the man sets up a situation so he can give himself permission to end the relationship. The man knows ahead of time he won't like the woman's response. Then, he confirms the inevitable: "I knew it would turn out this way."

    I went along with Ben's program to date others, and it surprised him. In fact, the night he informed me of his four-months-a-commitment agenda, I went straight out to a Great Expectations mixer; but before that, I reread the quote on my refrigerator door by Simone Weil, an early twentieth-century French philosopher:

> *Attachment is the great fabricator of illusions; reality can be attained only by someone who is detached.*

Maybe Ben thought he could stay away from me, but he kept coming back. At the end of the first year, he turned sixty and had a midlife crisis. He came to see me during the day, so I knew it must be important.

"Did you ever have one?" he asked.

He looked great. He'd lost twenty-five pounds by walking twenty-five miles a day. I wanted to call him Forrest Gump but didn't have the heart.

"A real nervous breakdown? No, not yet," I lied.

"Didn't you have one when you turned sixty?"

"Not that I know of," I said, feeling hopelessly in love because he was holding me so tight I thought I was going to die.

It was a fight for me to remember that he didn't want a woman in his life. I mean, come on, he used to sing the Henry Higgins song from *My Fair Lady!* "Let a woman in your life ..." Pretty clear, huh?

BLESS ME, FATHER, FOR I HAVE SINNED

I tried to put a positive spin on dating. At first I lacked the will, but then it was kind of interesting to meet all types of men coming in and out of my life for about six months. I had one more JDate, coffee with an attorney who wore high-waisted pants and rhapsodized about ballroom dancing, and I never dated on JDate again. Ben called and tease me about "high pants" and asked me if I was married yet; he was going to be in Santa Monica, and did I want to see him?

Love is a mystery, my therapist, Mike, told me. There is no rhyme or reason to its hold. One loves passionately or not at all.

Once again, Mike explained men to me: Ben's anima was in crisis because his mother complex was raging. Even at sixty, Ben had not been able to release himself or, more to the point, had not individuated, left home, completed a rite of passage so he could free himself to love completely. By the way, a bar mitzvah doesn't count as a defining rite of passage. It's not primitive enough. If only circumcision was done at puberty, then we'd have something to call a rite of passage.

Ben was a middle child and, as such, was a pleaser: he had caretaking commitments to his parents, he was busy making sailing documentaries with his producing partner, he was writing a one-man show with another woman, he was sailing in a race in San Diego. Ben used anything to block the possibility of surrendering to a loving relationship. He had always lived that way, even with his wife of twenty years. Ben was afraid that if a woman touched his soul, his protected sense of self would be destroyed. He told me he had been in love before he met me; but damn it, he wasn't going to endure another gut-wrenching ending, even though he had initiated the ending by not marrying the woman.

We would never end up together no matter how many times he returned to me by phone or to my apartment or under the Sherman Oaks sign on Sepulveda Boulevard. He could not give his soul to a woman.

I continued to yin and yang through the minefields of dating the male gender for another few months. The experience wasn't particularly enlightening in terms of my understanding of the male species. There were several men who were only out for the sport of sex or to confirm their fears that women were as greedy and materialistic as their ex-wives who received half their wealth in the divorce. By god, no woman was going to get what money they had left, except maybe they'd be blindsided by a hot thirty-five-year-old whose biological clock was ticking. That sad, angry rich guy didn't have a clue that the nymphet would eventually get half his wealth and 401(k) and a child to complete the perfect picture of wedded bliss or to extort more money in child support after the marriage failed.

There were other sixty-year-old men who couldn't possibly change their lives for a woman. They hoarded their money, kept their house off-limits, and wanted no disruptions in their daily routine. Comfort zones seemed inordinately important for these pathetic souls who didn't want anyone sharing their sandbox. They seemed somehow addicted to the dating game; after all, there was always an abundance of available women to date who flattered their egos and satisfied their sexual needs. These guys stayed online dating even when they were already committed in a relationship.

"Always keep your options open" was their mantra. I've known men who would never let their subscribing to dating services run out. There was a man I met who didn't even know if he was getting billed for the dating service and/or didn't even know how many services he had subscribed over the years. *And the man I'm referring to was seventy-five years old!*

Despite confirming evidence in so many of these cases that these men were unsuitable for me, and perhaps I for them, the pervasive mind-set in the Internet-dating universe is one of unconsciousness, the inability to connect true feelings and intent. The dating situation is a breeding ground for a whole lot of dysfunctional behavior, creating illusions or delusions of grandeur for both men and women.

The following is a representative sampling of the men I dated on the Internet in my age bracket, fifty-five to sixty-five years old. Although the view through this window has the flavor of a voyeuristic peep show, the picture does confirm a certain bizarre disconnect between men and women.

LET'S MAKE A DEAL

Stockbroker Date: Beverly Hills, early fifties. He was too young for me, but was handsome and a workout fanatic. We met at Starbucks on Beverly Glen and Mulholland Drive. I thought the date was for dinner. "What do you want to do?" he asked.

"I thought we were going to eat dinner," I said shyly.

"I've already eaten. I don't eat after five o'clock." It was already seven o'clock.

There was an unattractive deli next to Starbucks, so I suggested I get something to eat there. The glaring fluorescent lights bore down on us as I ordered a boring dry salad.

First question: did you lie about your age on your profile? I tried to be light and funny. "I think all women lie about their age."

"It's not good to start a relationship with lies. How old are you?"

I told you my lie would come back to bite me. We were done for the evening and for a lifetime. He paid for my salad. He only had water.

Writer/College Teacher Date: I met him at a mixer, and we hit it off. We went out three times to dinner. He asked me to spend New Year's Eve with him, but then he decided to go with friends to Thailand during the Christmas holidays. The tsunami hit. I thought he was dead. I didn't hear from him for two weeks. He returned—alive. But he was way too cool about the entire experience—water up to his chest, wading through dead body parts in the hotel lobby. Maybe he didn't want to emotionalize the experience. With even less emotion, he told me he wasn't going to see me anymore because we never talk about any subjects relating to him, such as playwriting, screenwriting, teaching, movies, art, and the like. That's all I remember talking about except to tell him about my family. I think all he wanted to talk about was my fishnet stockings and how sexy they were. We had dated only three weeks. I should have known better. He was never married, had no children, and smoked pot.

Music Producer Date: A very nice man and a gentleman. We dated twice, and then he told me I wasn't his type. He wanted to be fair with me, so he thought he should tell me as soon as possible that he was looking for a different kind of woman. However, he thought we had great chemistry. I thought we had no chemistry. The day after our second date, I got an e-mail from him telling me what a terrific woman I was and that I would surely find a good companion. I was relieved he did the dumping. He smoked a lot of dope too. I met him later at a party for Obama, and he didn't remember me but asked the hostess for my phone number.

Photographer Date: Really good at what he did. He traveled all over the world, lived in Bali, was spiritual, but was not in a good economic situation. I discovered there are men over sixty who have not prepared for retirement. There was a desperate quality to him, and I felt bad because I imagined at another time in his life, he was in a happier space. He became too needy, and I actually ended it. He got hostile and was not a gentleman. So much for Bali and the Buddhist lifestyle.

Business Industry Date: Fresh off a divorce and not the best kind of man to sit and have coffee with because he is thinking about how I was plotting to get his money. We had no chemistry at all. I found him completely offensive, braggart, insecure, pompous, and without a scrape of charm or dignity. I'm quite sure he found me boring, too old, and incapable of grasping how much money he had lost in his divorce. So, why go on insufferably about his house on Lake Tahoe, which he managed to keep for himself?

Insurance Industry Date: Four years after his divorce, he has discovered the freedom to be his own drug of choice. He just wanted occasional company for dinner. Whatever he chose to do, he preferred to do it by himself, as in hiking, or with his children, as in traveling. He kept telling me all the things he was doing, but not with me. Way too involved with his ex-wife's life. He was a true *puer,* never to be caught by a woman again. He wore a sign: don't get too close, I might fall apart. Unfortunately, he was my insurance agent. Thank God Medicare kicked in!

Public Relations Date: This was my favorite Internet date. We went out for several months and enjoyed each other's company. He was very smart and very kind. Two things made it challenging: I think he was looking for a younger woman, and he had a teenage daughter from a second marriage that he was overly devoted to. I also think his business was going through a transition, and he had more on his plate than he could handle. But during the time I was with him, I enjoyed his company. About eight months later, he called to find out if I was available because his relationship with another woman didn't work out. I was with the sociopath who was reading my e-mail. I hope the PR guy found someone to love again.

Salesman Date: He was from Minneapolis. He found me online while he was vacationing in Palm Springs. I was fine about developing a relationship with someone in another state. I had to go to Las Vegas to see my family; he had to go to for a convention. We met at the Bellagio. I had secured the reservation with my credit card. At the desk, I suggested he use his card instead of mine. He thought we were going to split the room. "No," I declared, "I'm treating you to Cirque du Soleil, and I'm renting a car." We did have fun. But there was a bit of the salesman in his personality, scoping out the territory, examining the goods; yet he was also warm and affectionate. When we checked out, I had to remind him that I held the room reservation with my credit card and had no intention of paying. Several weeks later, my credit card bill arrived. I had been charged for that first night. I called the salesman to tell him that I was charging the first night back to his credit card and to please verify it with the hotel. He stopped calling. Later, through a second party, I discovered he didn't think I had enough money. It seems my 401(k) wasn't up to his standards. He rode a Harley and had land in Montana, which was very attractive. But he was also overly devoted to his adult daughter.

Movie Marketing Date: He was kind of a strange man. I couldn't quite understand why he was Internet dating. He seemed somewhat complete in his work and his life. He was smart, chic, lived in Venice on my old street, right behind Muscle Beach. He rode a motorcycle and liked to hang out at James' Beach restaurant, and so did I. He had two daughters, one more beautiful than the other. Because he was also a photographer and had a terrific artistic sense, his home was beach cool. His last girlfriend was in her twenties, and this guy was in his midsixties or more. And then again, he was so devoted to his daughters that he fixated on them. He showed me artistic photo books devoted to their trips together. I couldn't even hope to compete. Last thing I heard was that he was taking one of his daughters, the most beautiful one, to Venice for the summer. He was really excited about their trip together.

I was definitely curious about fathers who are overly indulgent and overly involved in the lives of their adult daughters. I asked Mike about what I perceived to be an overly extreme closeness because I found it seemingly unhealthy and definitely creepy to watch fathers fixating on their adult daughters. While it was appropriate that a father would take great interest in his adult daughter, Mike suggested that overt devotion to a daughter, using her as his consort, was a way to protect the man from avoiding intimacy or falling in love. *Bingo!*

Real Estate Date: A perfectly nice gentleman whose profile and picture were absolutely nothing like he was in person. After three lunches, he told me that he got the result of his AIDS test; he then asked when I had last been tested. Enough said. He needed to learn the art of foreplay. I could have been too hard on this one.

Sicilian Date: I couldn't believe how handsome and fit he was. I usually go for guys whose mind and humor turn me on, and they are rarely pretty boys. I dated him for about a year and a half but tried to break up with him within the first year because he seemed overly possessive. But I was trying to stay away from connecting with Ben again, so I continued on with the Sicilian out of habit and sexual compatibility. The Sicilian was the only man I brought home to meet my family; he was my date at Aaron's wedding. Neither son liked him. There was always something sinister about his character, and it was reflected in his obsessiveness. I finally ended it, but not soon enough. What I didn't know was that the Sicilian had gotten into my e-mail by retrieving my password from his computer, and he had been reading everything I wrote for an entire year. I still feel the sleaze factor all over me.

MATCHMAKER, MATCHMAKER, MAKE ME A MATCH

I also read about speed dating, lunch dating, and finding your executive match dating. Some fees ran into the thousands. Finally, I ran across an article about a mother/daughter matchmaking service. I was intrigued. I called, and the daughter immediately asked my age.

"In your age-group, we don't have any available men," she told me. "Single men over sixty are at a premium."

But she took pity on me and told me to come in. Five minutes into the interview, I knew I was in the wrong place. I started to sweat through my armpits. Even though mother/daughter really thought I had terrific energy, there was no one they could think of that I might be right for. After an hour, I backed out the door and wondered if the matchmaking services in the nineteenth-century Russian shtetels were similar to what I went through. Too ugly? Too fat? Too skinny? Too old? Never too young. "Can't find a man for you, but we'll put you on file." I felt like a freak in a sideshow.

MOVIN' ON DOWN THE HIGHWAY

"Men are basically real estate," my friend Peter said the other day. "If you don't like the man, move on to the next. There is property available all over the city."

My Internet-dating experience and the subsequent series of blind dates I have had recently, while not exactly full of enlightenment, produced a few observations about men. This, of course, doesn't mean that I know any more about men than when I started dating. Anecdotal material can be useful for purposes of example; but more to the point, they can be experiential and revelatory for the person going through the experiences.

Dating men sixty and over is challenging because most men at this age are set in their ways. They are guarded when it comes to opening up the heart to love; like all humans, they fear the unknown, or they simply lack a generosity of spirit that might lead them to take a leap of faith and fall in love. A few of my blind dates seemed lonely and unaware of how to connect with a woman or they didn't understand how to "give and take" when communicating. A man might not want to connect with a woman because of the aging process—a man's energy slows down because of a loss of sexual potency as a by-product of decreasing testosterone. Perhaps some men have a mother complex that won't allow them to connect fully to their loving natures. Mike says any man who will not let a woman touch his soul is a man who will never find fulfillment in his life. On the other hand, it's possible there was no pheromone attraction between my blind dates and me. Possible and quite probable.

I am always curious about how couples regroup in their sixties after forty years of marriage. I know several couples in this category and have been privy to the intimate details of their long-term marriages. Several of the married women, in fact, have left their husbands, preferring to live single lives. Women in their late fifties and sixties indicated they need the company of men less and less and preferred the company of women friends. These newly single women felt more healthy and vigorous and even more independent than their male counterparts. Yet, the husbands—left to fend for themselves—suffered from confusion, failed to adjust to changes in routine, and felt depressed. Sometimes their health was impaired. While married men grew more dependent on their wives and cultivated fewer male friends, women felt a growing sense of freedom.

This seeming paradox between men and women produces some confusing behavior and can bring about conflicting emotions. As a man's sex drive decreases from the loss of testosterone, a woman's libido can increase after menopause. She can be sexually active into the sixties and seventies, even eighties. The imbalance of the sexes in later years affects a man's ego. The man's ego becomes more fragile, and as a woman's sense of self grows, she may look for a younger man.

SEARCHING FOR INTELLIGENT SIGNS
And that's how it has gone for me in the dating universe. My therapist didn't seem to feel that it was important that I gained any deep perspective about men. He said something more revealing to me.

"You still need to examine your relationship with your animus. A woman balances her anima, her feminine, with her masculine animus."

Why did I have to work on my masculine aspect?

It happened by accident one day when I was with Corinne, my barometer for my single angst.

"The man I'm looking for is already in me," I blurted out.

It was startling to me that I articulated such a concept. I was looking elsewhere for a man to complement my natural energies, to cherish me, to bring me joy. My animus was stuck inside of me, and as yet, I had no insight to the inner workings of its antecedents.

Emotions were clouding my consciousness because I still believed in the fantasy of the white knight rescuing the fair maiden. This fantasy is a curse to all women. At sixty-four, it was an old conceit that I should have lost decades before because I had always taken care of myself and just didn't know it. I had the Romeo and Juliet romantic love complex, but that pair of romantic lovers ended up dead.

It is difficult to let go of preconceived ideas based on old cultural and parental messages. I grew up with Mom wanting her daughter married and fulfilled. Translated: that means she finds a man and stays married for life, no matter the circumstances, and Mom doesn't have to worry about her anymore.

When I never remarried by the age of sixty-four, my mother finally gave up on the idea that I would ever be anything but a bohemian. One day, just before my mother turned ninety-six and had the inevitable fall, which began her descent into physical fragility and dementia, we had a brief conversation.

"Are you okay?" my mother asked me cryptically.

"I'm fine, Mom," I said gently. "I know how much you wanted me to find a man, but I think I've accepted my life as it is."

"Well," she said philosophically, "men don't make you happy anyway. I never wanted a man around after your father died. Just a lot of trouble ..."

What continues to make me smile is the ironic twist waiting just around the corner. Just after I turned sixty-five, two men approached me—at different times and places. Both were much younger (I think in their early forties) and, I might add, very handsome. One was a Whole Foods approach; the other was a Third Street Promenade approach. Both men told me they got a vibe from my energy. Imagine checking out apples in the produce section, and someone spots my energy. And the other man came up to me as I was wheeling my grandson down the promenade in Santa Monica. We talked for five minutes about yoga and the exchange of energy in the universe, and our eyes and bodies were alive with life.

I'm thinking about burying the white knight in Forest Lawn Cemetery. I am also pleased that I'm less compelled to look for love in all the wrong places. The beauty in life rests with my present joy and gratitude.

The men I've known and other sociopaths have contributed to the state of my well-being in significant ways: they made me grow, reflect, practice self-restraint, and raise the level of my awareness about who I am, where I am, and what I expect of myself. Just the other evening, I met a man at an Obama thank-you party. We had some chemistry going on. He gave me his Web site, I e-mailed him, and he e-mailed me back but didn't ask me out. So I asked him out electronically. And we went out, and it was easy and fun. Unfortunately, he had what I call the "master of the universe" complex, so it was his road or no road. He didn't want any obligation to me or to the relationship. I also quickly spotted the intimate father-daughter connection, but I gave it a go with dating for a time and then decided not to date him anymore. That was a baby step in the practice of self-mastery because I knew my needs were not being met. I was not afraid of moving on down the highway. That's living my life to the fullest and taking care of myself at sixty-five.

Text message from my brother
didn't u learn from Dad
men pay, women don't...
get a grip... at ur age
u should know better

CHAPTER 7
IS HE CHEAP, OR IS HIS HAND STUCK IN HIS POCKET?

I'm not going to generalize about how cheap or generous men are because each man is different. But the man who is generous with his money usually has a generous heart. Of course, there are exceptions: It could be fake generosity to impress, and in that case, the man is stealing affection without genuine feeling. Generosity could be based on power, as in "he who has the gold rules." This kind of giving arises from an inflated ego, and more often than not, it is a way to control the little woman. Disingenuous generosity based on guilt or a person's negative energy will eventually backfire on the giver. The receiver, on the other hand, might feel cheated out of genuine emotion; and something unpleasant is bound to happen.

Does a man really expect something for his financial generosity? If a man and a woman are in a committed relationship, there is a high probability that a man expects a woman to respond to his generosity by taking care of and fulfilling most of his personal needs, even professional requirements if that is applicable. Of course, we know women who are takers, and we know men who are only receivers. Neither flaw is attractive.

This is not to imply that a woman cannot be generous with her pocketbook if she has the will and the means to do so. I have known several women who take care of most of the financial needs of their men. It is clearly an unconventional reversal of what is expected in our society (think: men=hunter/gatherer). I was one of those women. I am a cursed overgiver, resulting from the need, I presume, to please. I'm also generous to a fault and ask for far too little in return.

Since the beginning of time, women have come to expect that men will pick up the tab and bring home the bacon. It has taken a couple of decades for me to discover that I don't have to be a full-time financial caretaker for the male gender if my pocketbook is on the light side. And who better to teach me this than my younger friends, women in their thirties, who make me promise that when I am confronted with a man's lack of financial acuity, take the high road and boogie on out of a potential quagmire. On the other hand, if I hear, "I'll fly you out next week, and we'll spend the weekend together," I'm good to go.

A FEW GOOD MEN

My role model for how men handle money was my father. I never thought men could have a problem with money because my father was very generous to everyone. My dad came from a poor Irish Catholic family with lots of kids. He lived in a working-class section of San Francisco called the Mission District. (It's chic to live there now.) No one in that family thought they were poor. My dad and I played a game when I needed money. On top of his dresser, he kept coins in a tray. In the top drawer, he kept the bills. He'd say, "Get what you need." I took what I needed for the movie or for an ice cream cone from the coin tray: twenty-five cents for the movie and ten cents for an ice cream cone. "Look in the top drawer."

"I'm okay, Daddy."

He'd say, "Take a fin. You never know when you might need it."

My brother learned very early how to be a truly generous soul too. See text message above. He has always been the most generous brother to me, and to this day, I trust him more than anyone. He was not pleased with me for my financial support of David, even though David was worth his weight in gold for his unending sweat equity on the fixer houses, for taking care of my sons, and for adding to my personal happiness. To his credit, David always had teaching gigs and diligently followed leads to make money. But the years took its toll on my finances, and my brother would just shake his head at me and tell me to protect myself better. There is that mystery of love again!

I went to high school from 1958 to 1961, and I cannot remember a time when I had to pay for any or all of a date. The boys had part-time jobs and worked summers to have spending money and take the girls out on weekends. The dating scene was integral to a high school boy's rite of passage. So maybe we split the bill for french fries and Cokes at the local hangout after school; but if it was a night date, at Mel's Drive-In or O' Sole Mio pizza parlor in the Marina after a movie, our dates picked up the tab. If we went to dinner in Sausalito before the junior prom or to the Fairmont Hotel before the senior ball, our dates always paid with a sense of pride. Was there any other way to take a girl out?

My favorite "generous men" stories took place in Vegas in the 1960s and 1970s. It's probably not kosher to say this, but those Mob guys I met through my ex-husband were some of the most generous men I have known. Okay, maybe there were other issues going on with these people like murder, extortion, money laundering, and racketeering; but I had no personal knowledge of these situations. The wise guys were always very respectful to me. I used to raise money for my theater from them, mostly upper hotel management and presidents and a few mob men. Every year, I would walk out of their hotels with contributions for my theater. The theater staff used to joke that the plaque in the theater lobby represented the Who's Who of the Las Vegas Mob. But when I was soliciting for donations, the wise guys escorted me to my car after treating me to lunch and paid for valet parking. They opened my car door and watched me drive off safely. At dinners with the Damon Runyon crowd hanging out at Caesars Palace in the Bacchanal Room, they were generous to a fault. They used to ask me to "say some Shakespeare, Joanie," and I'd fumble around with Ophelia's death scene. They loved my shtick even though I mutilated the lines.

Why do men lose consciousness when a woman is waiting for valet parking? Maybe when dinner is over, they think the date is over. My friend Peter wouldn't think of allowing a woman to pay for parking. The minute I show up for our sushi dinner on Saturday nights, he takes the parking ticket out of my hand, and I never have to think about it again. I don't even know how or when he pays for my parking; he is such a smooth operator. The moment is delicious.

Peter is the quintessential date. Happiness is the key to his generosity. He spends money and treats people well because it is his pleasure. For Peter, money has no strings. My son Jonathan is very much the same way. He is completely generous and picks up the tab more than he should. My ex-husband continues to be generous with family, and of late, he was extremely generous with me. Yes, my ex-husband—can you beat that? My sons are not always flush with money; maybe it's a bad year or a bad decade, but nevertheless, I've never seen men behaving badly with money in my family or with Peter and a few other generous men.

David had a huge heart and loved to spend money even when times were difficult. "They're still printing it" was the mantra. When he was working, he always treated me generously. Unfortunately, David's relationship with money was less than stellar, and his secretiveness was the root of our problems. He had an unconscious relationship with credit cards. It was just bad luck that money was his tragic flaw.

Recently, I had the most beautiful experience with true generosity. It was summer vacation in Newport/Balboa and Carli, Jonathan, my grandsons, and I were all dining together with a few friends and their families from Las Vegas.

"Scott picked up the tab," Jonathan said on the way out. "That was really generous."

I saw Scott signing the bill and went up to him to thank him personally. Scott is one of Jonathan's good friends. He is in his mid-thirties, a hard worker, and a family man who throws the most generous birthday parties for his kids. And he always wears a smile.

"It's my pleasure," he said joyfully. "I work so I can do these kinds of things, take care of people and make them feel good."

Scott truly understands the joy of being generous.

THE ART OF CHEAPOSITY

Why do some men get their hands stuck in their pockets when it comes to being generous with money? Some men even elevate cheaposity to an art form. I have actually witnessed men construct a vast array of dodges at the dinner table—fumbling with credit cards, trying to divide the bill, and asking their dates for cash handouts, causing female observers to visibly cringe. And this egregious behavior comes mostly from single or divorced men post fifty-five. I am curious as to why this phenomenon occurs.

A male friend of mine, age sixty-three, admitted to me that his cheaposity comes from his father who was stingy and who begrudgingly gave money to support his family. My friend never learned about the joys of generosity, so he never learned how to spend graciously. I first noticed my friend's cheaposity when he had difficulty offering to pay for a meal, either for me or for at least half the table. A couple of times, he paid for me; but other times, he was challenged by the prospect of paying, even when it was for a $6 burrito. He told me in an unguarded moment that when he was married, his wife paid half the mortgage every month even though he made a good living. Spending made him feel uncomfortable, and he didn't have a good relationship with money. He grew up poor and still felt poor as an adult. Although my friend recognized his father was a hoarder, he was unable to use money to make other people and himself happy. This man will always be a sad soul because it was so difficult to let go of his troubled heart.

Then there are those men who have significant wealth and who cannot give anything without feeling deprived. If they give, it takes away from their sense of self. These people are sad souls too, but of a different sort. Often wealthy men think that money is power; and they use money as a weapon against wives, children, and other family members, even parents. Sometimes the acquisition of money appears to be more important than spending it. No matter the circumstances, money is very often the central focus of discussion. Do I look like a bank? Why is everybody coming to me for money? I'm not going to share my money with another woman after my divorce. In these examples and perhaps more, cheaposity comes from a deprived soul, a psyche who lives in the shadow world of the unconscious. The heart has separated from the mind. A person who is cheap never sees the light and never opens a stubborn heart.

The Sicilian appeared generous and treated me nicely, as did another man who was my companion for a time; but the money spent on me was more to self-aggrandize, to establish a position with me, and was not given completely out of a generosity of spirit. The money spent didn't feel as if it came from an honest place in their hearts. The gesture implied, "What are you going to do for me now?" or "Stay at my side; don't read when I am with you on the beach," or "Look at what I spent on you; look at the wine I brought you, the meal I'm cooking for you, and this is what I get? How dare you break up with me?" Money doesn't buy love.

The topper cheaposity story, of course, was the incident at the Bellagio Hotel with Mr. Minneapolis. Prying a credit card out of a man to pay a hotel bill shows a man behaving badly, and besides, it's sleazy. I don't think I'll ever get over the look on his face when he tried to pull a fast one and let me pay for the hotel room at the Bellagio, and I nailed him. I guess he thought he deserved a cover charge for meeting me in Vegas even though he had a convention to attend. I guess he was wrong. What happens in Vegas doesn't always stay in Vegas.

A man's relationship with money comes in many sizes and shapes and can have multiple psychological levels. I think money is a complicated issue.

My theater friend lives on a fixed income. I have more disposable income than he does because I still work. I am happy to split the money for a movie and dinner. However, when I am with him, I find I am over-nurturing and give more for a dinner. I have a glass of wine, and he does not. When the bill comes, it is awkward. He reviews the check. Why I think he should split the bill and pick up half my wine just because he's a man could be a holdover from the fifties or sixties about how a man treats a woman. The bottom line is I don't have the patience to divide the check and do the math. If I have to figure the tip, forget about it. Keep the $20.

In the final analysis, Cher said it best: "If you don't take their money, you don't take their shit." You go, Cher.

A FEW BAD MEN

What a fascinating adventure it has been watching the relationship of men with their money. I will confess that I don't have a very good coping mechanism when it comes to money matters. It takes courage for me to simply observe and not take it personally. Easier said than done.

Dr. Demento and Ben were polar opposites on the money issue. They were both cheap but in different ways. Demento liked to spend on himself—on expensive restaurants, clothes, trips, and exquisite flowers. He never bought my ticket to fly to his city, but he gave me a few gifts along the way as a thank you for staying with me in Los Angeles and chauffeuring him around town. Of course, the night he broke up with me, I meticulously gathered every gift he gave me and threw them in the trash, with the exception of an exquisite black thong with beautiful red roses running up the front panel. I'm not a complete idiot! Yes, I bought the ticket to NYC; but when Demento wanted to know if I would pick up half the room at the Chelsea Hotel in New York City, I absolutely refused to pay anything.

"How could a man ask that of a woman?" I sputtered.

"Then you can pay the train tickets to Upstate," he countered.

It was obvious that he should pay. We were visiting his mother!

However, when Demento had a preliminary fantasy about moving in together in his home, he asked if I would be willing to pick up half the mortgage. I had to remind him it was his house and not mine. Remember the old saying "What's mine is mine, what's your is yours, and what's yours is mine too"? Is that still applicable these days?

Ben was different, but his cheaposity carried some of the same dysfunction. For some strange reason, he wanted me to get a mini-washer for my apartment so I wouldn't have to do full loads in the laundry room. It was a hand-crank job used on boats.

"Are you going to buy this for me, Ben?" I asked nonchalantly.

"No," he replied bluntly.

"Really? You want me to buy this $50 oversized plastic eggshell for my apartment, and you won't buy it for me?"

"Yeah, you're gonna love it. Think of the money you'll save doing laundry," he said with excitement.

To impress, I bought the damn thing and regretted it. And that offensive white Easter egg went in the trash too. Every time I looked at it, even when I tried to hide it, I knew it was in my apartment; and I was furious.

The top Ben cheaposity story occurred the last time we were out together. It had been seven months since I heard from him.

INT. JOAN'S APARTMENT - DAY
INTERCUT JOAN and BEN on the phone in his car.

                    BEN
        How are ya?

                    JOAN
        Fine. And you?

                    BEN
        Great.

                    JOAN
        Good.

                    BEN
        I miss you.

                    JOAN
        Why?

                    BEN
        I just miss you.

> JOAN
> You miss the kibitz.

> BEN
> I miss you.

I didn't budge for three weeks. I was very proud of myself, but still confused. I went back to therapy.

INT. THERAPIST'S OFFICE - DAY
JOAN sits across from MIKE in his office.

> MIKE
> Maybe you should tell him you love him.

> JOAN
> (in upper vocal register)
> What! You've got to be kidding!

> MIKE
> I'm not. That's what you should do.

> JOAN
> You're not supposed to tell me what I should do.

> MIKE
> That's right. But this time, I'm telling you what you should do.

> JOAN
> Why?

                    MIKE
            Because you love him.

                    JOAN
            Okay, I still love him.

                    MIKE
            Tell him.

                    JOAN
            I can't.

I called Ben and told him I loved him. It was bad timing. He was in the car with his son on the way to the airport.
 "I'll call ya back," he said with a lilt in his voice.
 I sat on the couch holding my breath until he called me back.

INT. JOAN'S APARTMENT - DAY
INTERCUT JOAN and BEN on the phone.

                    BEN
            I'm not the same old Ben.

                    JOAN
            Yes, you are, Ben, same old and
            confused Ben.

                    BEN
            I promise I'm not.

                    JOAN
                  (pauses)
            I have two tickets to Jersey Boys
            at the Ahmanson. Want to go?

BEN
Are you still with that good-looking guy? Is his picture still on your bookcase?

JOAN
I broke up with him two weeks after I told you to go peddle it elsewhere. Remember, I asked you if you were ever going to open your heart to me and you said no. The picture's gone.

BEN
I didn't say that.

JOAN
You turned on your heels, whistling an unhummable tune and marched down the stairs. You reminded me of one of the Seven Dwarfs singing, "Heigh-ho, heigh-ho, it's off to work we go …"

BEN
(casually)
Yeah, I'll go with you.

JOAN
(snapping at Ben)
Don't do me any favors, Ben.

BEN
No, I really want to go. I mean it, pussycat. I want to see you.

We went together to a play just like when we first began our strange odyssey. I was always in heaven with Ben. We sang old songs, laughed at each other's jokes, found each other's hands and arms, fed each other, and sipped out of each other's drinks. After the show, we walked into the lobby past the CD booth. I loved the show and the music and Frankie Valli because it reminded me of high school. I wanted to buy the CD.

"You can get it cheaper on Amazon," he said as he tried to lead me out the front doors.

"It's $20! I want to play it in the car driving home," I said vehemently.

"But it's cheaper on Amazon," he quickly shot back.

I forgot to mention that Ben is a very, very rich man, but you'd never know it. I left the theater without the CD. Bile was coming up in my throat, spilling out my ears, flowing through my nose; and I wanted to scream out to anybody listening. How could I love a man with a defective heart? How was it possible?

Love is a mystery. Well, you can have your damn mystery!

My love affair was ending. I made dinner for Ben after the theater. The fish tacos were dry. The evening was predictable. He spent the night, even staying in bed while I left at six in the morning to teach my yoga client. When I returned, he was gone, but the bed was made. I didn't hear from him all week. It was the same old Ben.

I was house sitting for my son in Venice when Ben called. He was on his way to defrost the icebox on his boat, and he asked me to join him on the boat.

I lacked enthusiasm, but I went to the boat. Good old Ben! I ruined my nails by scrubbing rust off the ladder all afternoon. We didn't talk much, which was unusual for us. As we chipped away at the crusted ice inside the sailboat's icebox, I found myself staring at him. The silence made him look at me.

INT. BEN'S BOAT - AFTERNOON
BEN and JOAN are cleaning the icebox on
his boat. Ben looks up at Joan staring at him.

>BEN
>What is it? You're looking at me
>funny.

>JOAN
>You're used to women giving you
>things, offering you perks like a
>yacht or a trip to the Hamptons;
>and you don't feel the need to
>give back, do you?

>BEN
>(studies her face)
>That's right.

We finished defrosting, shopped at Ralph's for his fried chicken and my salad, listened to 60 Minutes on the radio, ate in silence, made love in silence, and then said good-bye in the marina parking lot. It was finally over between us, but it was never going to be over in my heart. Love is damn mystery!

I AM WOMAN: HEAR ME ROAR

Since I am a woman who grew up in the 1950s and 1960s, I am accustomed to men who treat woman with chivalry. In those decades, a father taught his son how to be a man in the presence of a woman.

Cut to the 1970s, and the feminist movement was in full swing. Women demanded their rightful share of the professional pot. I even hit the glass ceiling at the university where I taught and witnessed the first female professor sue for tenure in the English department.

I postulate—without any basis in research, mind you—that men's evolving cheaposity began several years after the women's movement. As women acquired more money, prestige, and equal protection under the law, they lost some perks in the transition of gaining full independence alongside men. By the 1980s, it became de rigueur for women to pay for themselves and occasionally pay for the man for dinner and maybe a movie if she felt like treating or if she made more money than the man. It was cool and trendy for the woman to be in the driver's seat.

I'm as guilty as any of those over-nurturing women who have been independent for so long that I expect I'll pay my part and more of a bill. I am always appalled at myself when I do. It seriously irks me when a man in my group fumbles to pay the bill or looks at me as if to say, "Aren't you going to pay your share?" I have participated in more of these incidents than I'd like to admit. I'm so used to it now that I write it off to unsportsmanlike behavior.

Both genders have been complicit in signing off on this new economic parity so that in time, male/female boundaries have been blurred. Both genders are angry at each other because social conventions are ill defined, and neither gender knows how to communicate their unrealized expectations when it comes to finances.

As men witness the "equal rights" show, they view women with knowing smiles of complicity; it is the women's obligation to pay their fair share since the women's movement proffered the new paradigm. Maybe some men believe themselves to be entitled to a cover charge because they provide companionship and sex, or their resentment against the women's movement is so unconscious that they forget to open a car door for a woman or let her walk back to her car alone; or they step ahead of a woman in line, don't hold the door open for her, flip her off on the freeway for any driving infringement, yell at her at a stoplight because she does not move quickly enough when the signal changes. It is unfortunate that I have encountered all of the above. I recognize the rudeness with a sense of sadness.

Naturally, women counter by playing obstructive and rude games with men. Now, for example, a woman flips a man off or yells obscenities when she is cut off on the 405 Freeway, mimicking the male behavior. The rules of the gender game have changed, and it isn't for the better. There is little respect on both sides.

A man's relationship to money is downright complicated and sometimes dysfunctional. Maybe it has to with hoarding for the next cold winter. Or more often than not, a man has not prepared for a sensible retirement, and money will always be a huge problem. Taking early social security will provide little financial security for future decades. It's all scary. In any event, most of us will outlive our money, so we might as well enjoy what we have in the present.

MADE IN AMERICA

When speaking to several of my women friends about this chapter on cheaposity, they all chimed in, "It's only American men who are cheap." You'd never catch a Latin man not paying for a woman at dinner. Even the young kids in other cultures, specifically the Middle Eastern cultures, never allow a lady to pay. Unfortunately, European men mimic their American counterparts. I can recall several outings with German and Dutch men who wouldn't think of offering to pay for a woman. And I've witnessed several German women throwing down money on the dinner table and stomping out of the restaurant.

I remember an inspirational lunch in Buenos Aires in a small restaurant behind the huge shopping promenade known as Calle Florida. An older man I met at a *milonga* asked me to lunch one afternoon with some of his friends. We met before the luncheon at a *confitería* for an espresso. He was quite a famous artist in Argentina, and we had a lively discussion about art and literature before heading out to the restaurant. As we strolled into a side alley, he explained to me the particulars of the people who would be gathering for lunch: there would be about ten fellow artists and friends from around the city.

Lunch was in progress as we arrived. I happened to be one of two women at the table. The guests were all distinguished artists—brilliant, creative, graceful, funny, and spirited. They ordered sumptuous food and wine, Argentine beef, salads, and papas fritas; and it was never in question that I would be treated, feted, and embraced as part of that illustrious community. I would never see any of these men again, but the memory endures.

We will never know whether the cheapness of some American men is a result of the quirks of advanced age, damaged psyches, stinginess or rudeness, resentment over women getting their full rights, a cultural disposition, character flaws that evolve out of parental models, or a bad divorce. But when we are confronted and confounded by these attitudes and disposition, we must always remember: it's only money, and they're still printing it. Thank you, David.

Text message from my friend Annie
will never speak to u if u
have sex w him before 3rd
date rule play hard to get
don't care if he has the best
dick ever but did u see it yet?

CHAPTER 8
THONGS I HAVE WORN

I don't remember the exact moment when I decided to switch to a thong from traditional white underwear. I only remember how for decades I was sick and tired of looking at panty lines under my slacks. I wore white underpants until I was twenty-five. Of course, those were the times; today, full on white undies are hard to find. I was thirty when I switched to string bikinis, and that was because I was having children, and it was just more comfortable.

I bought my first thong at Victoria's Secret, but they proved to be an acquired taste. At first, it was challenging to wear them. I only wore them on special occasions, and then I pulled and tugged at my derrière like I had an attack of poison oak. Boy, I hated that string thong! Worst idea ever. How can anyone have a string ride up the butt all day?

In an effort to commit to the thong way of life, I kept going back to Victoria's Secret on field trips, scouring through the panty bins in search of the perfect thong. The salesgirls at Victoria's Secret hovered around me like mother hens, making suggestions and highlighting the various trendy aspects of wearing a thong. I tried out other styles. Some had a wide lace band around the hips that rolled up into a ball when I poured myself into tight jeans. It felt like toilet paper was sticking to the skin. I finally found the thong that was perfect for me, and then they discontinued the style. This has happened to me several times, but I am undaunted. I never pass a Victoria's Secret store without going inside.

My secret desire was to wear expensive bras, but I was reluctant to indulge. Low self-esteem is a killer when it comes to spending money on myself, especially if it doesn't show. My bras were, to say the least, utilitarian. But one day not long ago, while I was in Nordstrom—what else?—shopping for bras, I passed a rack of beautiful black and red lacey bras with a delicate bodice. I said, "What the hell?" and grabbed a black lace off the rack. I nervously tried it on in the dressing room. I knew I would like it even before I hooked it in the back. I was euphoric.

Historically, most cultures, including our own, glorify beautiful women in all states of dress or undress. My Catholic mantra of "modesty first!" was on its last leg. I bought the $100 Chantelle black bra! And even if no one else sees it, I know how it feels and looks on my body.

I'VE GOT YOU UNDER MY SKIN

Undergarments are utilitarian, but they are more than that. They can be beautiful, and I still want to feel beautiful and sexy at sixty-four. I think every personal choice we make affects our sensual sense of self. It feels fabulous to look our best even if clothes cover the red lace bra. And men love to feel and look good too, although they are not so obvious about it, except in Argentina and Italy where men dress and look better than women on any given day of the week. My belief is that we are never too old to feel sensual or to think about sex when the subject wraps itself around our minds. However, it has occurred to me that I probably think about sex more than anyone should at my age.

Contrary to sexual mythology, my sex drive didn't completely deteriorate when I went through menopause. When I didn't feel like having sex because of hot flashes, night sweats, and—surprise!—the dry vagina, an indication of plummeting estrogen, I investigated several over-the-counter lubricants. I liked Astroglide the best because it wasn't greasy, left no stains on the sheets, was fun to play with, and not a bit embarrassing to buy. Astroglide is even creative to use while having sex anytime, menopause or not.

I also found a natural, herbal product for menopause called Change-O-Life, which reduced the intensity of my flashes. I loaded up on magnesium too. Later, I mainlined estrogen vaginally because I was losing my boobs, and my skin was drying out. I had a tug-of-war with my gynecologist about hormone replacement therapy, but I succumbed to his arguments to take HRT; and my estrogen levels and sex drive came back with a vengeance, along with better skin, hair, and boobs. That was the beginning of my thong journey. I also took up Argentine tango, and that really made me feel sexy. I was beginning to feel nineteen again.

I'M TOO SEXY FOR MY UNIFORM

In the late 1950s and early 1960s, there were religious taboos against premarital sex not only in the Catholic faith, but there were also social taboos in the culture at large. The Puritan idea of sexual repression is alive and well and living in America, although most of the population seems not to adhere to the authoritarian bent on the subject of sex. However, my relationship with sex was conflicted because it was closely tied to my religion. I was too often reminded that sex was bad for my spiritual well-being, sex outside marriage was a sin, and sex was only meant for procreation. I was confused and resentful, because I intuitively knew that sex was part of the living experience. But as we all know, religious dogma harangues about the dark side of sex and stunts us with fear of intimacy, which precludes any natural experimentation.

I once read that sexual repression is at the root of all problems: *without sexual freedom, there is no self.*

I began having difficulty staying on track with the Catholic message when I started to neck with Ronnie Denman in the back row of the Rafael Theater in the fifth grade. I was enjoying my sense of self at a young age. My father influenced me with his liberal Catholic attitudes and a lack of Catholic guilt. I may be exaggerating, but Irish Catholics seem to make up their religion as they go along. By the time the children leave home, Sunday's church ritual deteriorates into a long bacon-and-egg breakfast without the mass. I morphed into a very liberal Irish Catholic.

Staying on track in my coed Catholic high school was even more difficult. Although boys and girls did not attend classes together, adolescent hormones floated around the schoolyard like seagulls skimming the ocean and diving for food. At recess, boys and girls raced toward each other like bees swarming the hive. It's not hard to imagine the proliferation of sexual innuendos passing between sex-starved adolescent boys and girls in ten-minute increments.

SEARCHING FOR JACK KEROUAC

Growing up, the most important interaction between adolescent boys and girls was social and built on friendship. Double-dating was common on weekends and our destination was always the thirty-minute drive to San Francisco where our destination was North Beach. We began our adventure at the corner of Columbus and Broadway. First up was the Condor Club, famous for the swing dangling over the huge round bar. Every night, Carol Doda performed naked on the swing, tormenting the men below her as they marveled at her amazing XXXX breasts.

It was inconceivable to imagine a more exciting and seductive atmosphere than North Beach, except perhaps for the Village in New York. There was Enrico's Sidewalk Cafe where the hip, cool beatniks hung out; the Purple Onion, where I saw the Kingston Trio and Mort Sahl; the Hungry I, where comedian Lenny Bruce shocked the country with his obscenity rant; City Lights Bookstore, where Lawrence Ferlinghetti read his poetry, Allen Ginsberg rocked the intelligentsia with his epic poem Howl, and where, for a brief moment, Jack Kerouac was a fixture. I saw my first transvestite show at Finnochio's and heard live jazz for the first time outside Basin Street West. We were teenage hipsters on the prowl for the unconventional, the bizarre, and all things that made us cool and hip.

It was the most exciting time and place to be teenagers. As in every rite of adolescent passage, our activities had particular rituals. When we hung out in the city with boys, we considered ourselves part of the Beat Generation and progressive freethinkers. We gave only passing notice to the homosexuals living in the hills above

North Beach because we were much more interested in politics and how John Kennedy was going to be our next president because Ike was old and boring. After dates, we'd drive to the ocean where the old Fleishhacker Zoo was still a fixture. Or we'd park under the Golden Gate Bridge and listen to jazz or Elvis or Chuck Berry on the radio and make out or watch the boys drink beer. We felt so grown-up until we realized that it was two in the morning, and we'd better get home and have a good excuse for being out so late. Everyone was going to get in trouble and be put on restriction, except me. It never occurred to my mother not to trust her daughter.

"Please don't wake me up when you get home," she announced when I started to drive in cars with boys.

LIKE A VIRGIN

By the time most girls had finished their first year in college at UCLA, the status of being a virgin no longer had relevance. I knew that girls in my sorority house experimented with sex, and they were on the road to finding a senior to marry by the time they finished college. Prior to my entering the university, I had wanted to become a nun, join the Maryknoll missionaries, and convert the pagan babies. However, my high school speech teacher and mentor, Father Cummins, a priest who had Jack Kennedy's good looks and élan, encouraged me to go to college and forget about my nun vocation. He read me like a book. He must have known that sex was on my mind.

By the end of my first year in college, I was actually looking for a way to end my virginity vigil. At the time, I didn't necessarily connect sex with love or marriage. "Really like" was good enough reason for me to have sex. Miraculously, when the sex hormones kicked in, guilt seemed to vanish.

Jack was tall, gorgeous, sexy, smart, funny; and did I mention sexy? We went out for several months, and I was smashingly in lust. I determined that he was going to be the man who was going to take my virginity. It was New Year's Eve, 1962, and Jack suggested we should get a room at a motel in Manhattan Beach. I considered myself lucky to get a jump start on the sexual revolution.

BERKELEY IN THE 60S

I transferred from UCLA to Berkeley less than a month after Jack and I seemingly had fallen in love. I wanted more personal freedom (the rules of the sorority house didn't do it for me), and I craved more of an academic challenge from my theater major. It was Berkeley in the sixties! That rarified atmosphere had a significant and profound influence on all of us who breathed in its liberal vibrancy. Being at Berkeley in the sixties was a badge of honor. We lived in a place and time that was ripe for experimentation. You could smell pot at every party. There were wild gatherings and mixed-race couples, and the coffee shops reeked of intellectualism. A month after I arrived on campus, I met my soon-to-be husband. He was a law student at Boalt Hall, an intellectual who was curious and sexy in that Jewish way I always fell for.

One night, I took my law school boyfriend home with me to San Rafael. It was late, and he slept on the couch in the den. My dad came downstairs and saw him sleeping.

"Who's the beatnik on the couch?" he asked as he poured himself a cup of coffee.

"He's my boyfriend," I replied casually.

"Tell him to get his ass up and move his motorcycle from behind my car."

I knew I had chosen the right man.

Why I stopped being a beatnik and got married when I was twenty is still a mystery to me. When my friends asked me, I simply said, "He rode up on a motorcycle, and it took my breath away. I'm a sucker for motorcycles." That's about as much thought as I put into it—except it was Berkeley in the sixties, and he was the second man I had sex with, and I was crazy in love.

Then Kennedy was shot; and the world as we knew it, the promise of the sixties died painfully on the Berkeley campus on November 22, 1963. And our generation was suddenly older, no wiser, and maybe less important or more important depending on how you view the boomer generation. In the next decade, we morphed into hippies, antiwar protestors, flower children, radical government-hating elitists, and pot-smoking commune dwellers that tried to follow our dharma.

Father Cummins didn't even blink when I asked him to marry me. And my Jewish husband didn't have to take religion classes or promise to raise his kids Catholic, but he did have to kneel in front of a crucifix that hung above the altar in Mission San Rafael as Father Cummins married us. He almost tore my chic Jackie Kennedy pillbox hat off my head.

"You owe me one," he angrily said under his breath, referring to his kneeling position and the big smile I carried on my angelic face.

The next thing I knew, I was living in Las Vegas behind the Flamingo Hotel in a cheap apartment building populated with hookers and a few pimps. I missed the Free Speech Movement, the Vietnam War protests, and the bra-burning feminists. I was in Dante's third ring of hell. Real life had passed me by because I fell in love.

IT'S VEGAS, BABY, VEGAS

To be fair, my ex had mentioned the potential of working in Las Vegas before he graduated from law school. I pretended not to hear it. I thought he was just musing on job prospects. The move became a huge bone of contention after three months of marriage. I begged my ex to stay in San Francisco and practice law so I could finish my last semester at Berkeley, get my PhD in theater, and be the university professor I always wanted to be.

```
INT. KITCHEN, BERKELEY FLAT - MORNING
JOAN and her EX are talking heatedly.

                    JOAN
          I don't understand your rea-
          soning. You go to law school in
          Berkeley because you wanted to
          practice in the city.
```

              EX
I never said that I wanted to
work in San Francisco.

              JOAN
You didn't? I thought that's what
we planned.

              EX
No, that's what you planned. I
always wanted to go back to Vegas. I've got more opportunities
to make money there. It's a wide-open town.

              JOAN
You knew I wasn't going to like
this. You're at the top of your
class. You could get a job at any
firm.

              EX
Jews don't get hired in San Francisco.

              JOAN
What do you mean? It's 1964, for
God's sake!

              EX
The city is still anti-Semitic.

              JOAN
How do you know that's true?
Did you take a poll? Got any statistics?

                    EX
It's full of Irish and Italians. All
Gentiles. Don't you get it? Yeah, I
might get a job, but I won't ever
make partner.

                    JOAN
But you're brilliant and—

                    EX
This is the way it is. I can get
a job with a top firm in Vegas.
I worked for this law firm last
summer. It's a done deal.

It was a natural fit for my ex to set down roots in Las Vegas. He had contacts in the city from his father and from working in the DA's office and a prestigious law firm during summer vacations. It was a disaster for me. I always had naturally curly hair. After three months in Vegas, my hair went straight, and the light in my eyes went out. There was nothing in Las Vegas except gambling casinos, cowboys, Sears and Penny's, and slots in grocery stores. I thought my ex had lost his mind. And I was sure I was going to lose my soul.

My marriage didn't resemble any of my fantasies, sexual or domestic. We were an old couple before we got to experience being a young couple. I don't think my ex-husband was ever a child. Responsibility was thrust upon him early in life, and he was an adult before he was eight years old. He was a compulsive worker who focused on making money. I assumed personal responsibility at a young age, but I still wanted to play. I thought for at least the first three years, we'd be in bed making love every moment we weren't working or studying. I didn't completely understand that my husband was a workaholic until the summer of 1964 when he studied for the Nevada bar in twelve-hour shifts. He got me a job at the Sahara Hotel, and we never saw each other long enough to become each other's best friend or even meet up in bed together at the same time.

SEND IN THE CLOWNS, THERE OUGHT TO BE CLOWNS

Maybe the influences of my youth and my personal sensibilities were too ingrained, and marriage was a long detour that left me in an unconscious state. I think I will always be that girl at Berkeley in the 60s—a natural free spirit that just happened to be living in the oxymoronic town of Las Vegas, marching to my own drum, going against convention, against the grain of the institution of marriage. Even though I lived in a very big house and had all my creature comforts met, I was going through the motions of being married.

For a time, I was amused by dinners with the wise guys, the Damon Runyon crowd my ex and his partner represented. But after a while, I grew tired of talking about where the bodies were buried, my ex's unrelenting business trips and deals, his flakey associates, country club rituals, and, most of all, being a wife and mother without a husband's emotional support. My dreams for a stable home environment were falling apart, or maybe stability was never there.

I should have left my marriage years before, when my ex wanted my son Aaron to be born in Mexico City so he could own land in his son's name. This was the payback for his kneeling before a crucifix on our wedding day. Waiting in Mexico City's immigration office to get out of the country with my newborn typified the crisis in values in my marriage. I tried to work with what I had come to expect as a feeling of abandonment, of a lack of love and warmth, of cherishing and caring for each other; but the relationship issues were too profound to ignore. It was not just my relationship with my ex that was the ongoing problem; my mother's dysfunction with my alcoholic father impacted my fragile state. I perceived myself as a girl/woman who had never found her spiritual center. I needed the space to create my own life.

However, when I moved to Southern California, my plans went awry, and I found that I was an untethered soul led astray by the vagaries of an unfamiliar environment. Los Angeles without children that first year left me adrift while I waited to go to film school. I partied with friends on the Sunset Strip and waded through an atmosphere of genuine anonymity. It was all bad karma until I met

David; and life began to follow a path that most of the time made sense, except for our chosen career, which was always fraught with rejection.

When David and I dissolved our relationship and the Internet-dating splurge ended, there was no sign that love would ever resurface. My thongs and bras got more expensive, and my expectations of men in or out of the bedroom diminished.

When I awoke the day I turned sixty-four, I had few coherent thoughts. Of course, sex came to mind, followed by the desire to find a loving partner again. Another learning curve was ahead of me.

THE ART OF THE DEAL

There is an elephant in the room. Men and women reach sexual peaks at different ages in different decades. No one talks about that phenomenon. Young men peak sexually between nineteen and twenty-five; young women begin to peak between twenty-eight and thirty-five. Thereafter, there is a cooling-off period for both when couples are raising children, singles are unable to find a mate, or work becomes the dominant focus. Women begin menopause anywhere from forty-six to fifty-four. Men are still sexually active; and women, because of estrogen depletion, usually don't care about having ongoing sex. Then, when menopause ceases, a woman can get her sexual mojo going again while a man's loss of testosterone accelerates about midfifty. When a woman is ready to jump on the sexual bandwagon again, the man's sexual libido decreases. There's the rub, the problem, the biological moment of truth.

One day, while having a "nooner," for example, or one night after drinking too much or even not drinking too much, the woman and obviously the man notice that the man's erection isn't quite what they both had expected. The penis takes longer to get hard or goes soft upon entry into the vagina, or the penis doesn't get hard again—I mean again for the rest of the night after the man has ejaculated, or he might not even reach a climax. The woman is disappointed, unfulfilled, frustrated. The woman tries to take it in stride. The man is tired. He drank too much. He's thinking of another woman. But she is naked and feeling desirable. She knows there are other sexual options. He's too tired to care. He falls asleep.

The oftentimes "go to" recourse for sexually satisfying a woman is oral sex. I presume every man must know how to perform oral sex on a woman, although not all men like it. Oral sex is an enjoyable way for some women to be sexually satisfied in any decade of her life, especially when both genders are challenged by hormonal changes. There is also the option of using a hand or vibrator. If a woman wants more sex and there is no further sexual activity forthcoming, a woman may feel vulnerable. Yet, there are times, however, that a woman can be satisfied without having an orgasm, but not all the time.

The man leaves the bed and goes to the bathroom to relieve himself. The woman is lying in bed, wondering how to broach the subject of getting her needs met. She would like to have an orgasm, but she doesn't want to make the man feel bad. She rationalizes that he may not even know she didn't have an orgasm. The forty-year-old might sprout another erection, but the sixty-year-old most often cannot go another round, the Viagra wore off, or, worse, he forgot to take the Viagra and thinks he got away with faking it. Who gets sexually satisfied in these situations?

Solving this problem is relatively simple. It involves a sexual code for men and women while engaging in sex: *the man satisfies a woman first*. This should be obvious to a man, but to an unconscious man, that concept is not applicable. There's the rub, as Shakespeare would suggest.

INT. BEDROOM - NIGHT
Two candles burn on the side table. A beautiful sixty-year-old WOMAN is lying naked on a bed. Her body is in good shape. She stares at the ceiling.

A MAN, sixty-two, enters the room, drying off with a towel. He starts to get dressed.

MAN
I've got to get up early tomorrow to call Europe.

WOMAN
You're leaving?

MAN
I told you that I couldn't stay the night.

WOMAN
We never discussed that.

The man is fully dressed and is putting on his shoes.

MAN
Oh, we didn't? Okay, well, I can't stay anyway.

WOMAN
Is this it, then? You get off, and I don't.

MAN
You didn't get off? Why didn't you say something?

WOMAN
I thought you knew.

MAN
(laughs defensively)

Sorry about that. But you had
fun. I mean you sounded like you
had fun.

                    WOMAN

A little afterglow. A little spoon-
ing. Something more would be
nice.

                    MAN

Next time, I'll spend the night.

                    WOMAN

I don't think there'll be a next
time.

                    MAN

There's always something with
you broads. There's no satisfying
you.

Man leaves the room and slams the front door.

    The first time I realized that there was a recurring problem with a man's penis, I was in my forties, and he was in his late forties. The long-distance relationship had potential for long-term commitment. It was Thanksgiving in Nantucket. The situation occurred once before when we were in Aspen, but I thought it was performance anxiety. "Oh, that's fine, honey, don't worry. It's no big deal. We'll try later." And I hugged and kissed him and felt so sorry for him until it happened again in New Orleans after he asked me to marry him on the banks of Lake Pontchartrain. We were in a romantic setting in the French Quarter.

INT. BEDROOM, FRENCH QUARTER - DAY
WILLIAM and JOAN are lying naked in bed.

JOAN
Do you want to talk about this?

WILLIAM
What do you want to talk about?

JOAN
You asked me to marry you, but I don't know why.

WILLIAM
Of course, you do. I love you ...

JOAN
It's obvious. We have a sexual issue.

WILLIAM
No, we don't.

JOAN
I think we do. Has this happened with other women?

WILLIAM
It could be performance anxiety, but no, not really.

JOAN
What about with women before me or with women now?

> WILLIAM
> I saw a woman in New York …
> before you.
>
> JOAN
> And you were fine with her?
>
> WILLIAM
> I didn't have a problem with her.
>
> JOAN
> Are you still seeing her?
>
> William does not answer. Joan
> gets up, and enters the bathroom.
> She is distraught.

Then, there was the Viagra incident. The date in question was a man who had prostate cancer. I went out with him for several months, and it seemed the right time for sexual intimacy to occur. We went to breakfast with the intent to spend the day together. He told me that he did not take his Viagra that morning. He explained to me that it takes about an hour or two for the pill to take effect. I was unaware of the protocol. I didn't know what I was supposed to do until the Viagra kicked in. What topics of conversation would be appropriate to talk about while we waited for his penis to get hard? I asked him why he didn't take the pill before breakfast. He didn't have an answer. We tried again another time. It was awkward again.

It dawned on me that there must be a more artful way of handling sex at sixty, and it's called conversation, which might lead to a fulfilling sexual experience for both the man and the woman if they are open and honest about their sexual needs.

I recently heard a story from a male friend of mine about one of his male friends who was in a state of shock that his erections were becoming difficult to manage. "I don't get hard as often," he told my friend. My friend, on the other hand, has had prostate cancer for over fourteen years and was handling the situation with intelligence, very effective medication, and good communication skills with women. When men negotiate their sexual needs with women, women appreciate the candor and honesty. It's a turn-on, and everyone achieves the desired end. After all, we're sixty, and we've got to get over it.

A very good male friend who is seventy-eight years old has a very active sexual life. He dances tango every night of the week and goes to Buenos Aires three times a year. Of course, he takes Viagra. He wants a sex life. He's even experimented with Cialis, another prescribed sexual stimulant for men, which lasts longer and is somewhat easier to use if the man knows that he will be having sex over an extended period of time. This man was open, honest, and informative about his sexual activity with a number of women over a period of years. He told me that it was important to extend the foreplay when one takes the drugs, that physical stimulation promotes the erection and that the longer the foreplay, the better.

Discussion of sex and sexual intimacy in the sixties is an important component of shared affection. It is also clear that following a healthy lifestyle reduces stress and promotes a positive outlook on life. Greater understanding of the physical and emotional dynamics between men and women in the later years of life gives men and women the opportunity to take care of each other's intimate needs and desires.

SEX WITH BENEFITS: NO EXPIRATION DATE NEEDED

There was an informative article in the *Los Angeles Times*, November 17, 2008, entitled "Longer Lives, with Benefits." Regina Nuzzo, a freelance writer, reported that there was a silver lining when it came to aging. Ms. Nuzzo referenced a 2004 study at the University of Chicago in which researchers at the National Social Life, Health, and Aging Project set out to study the sex lives of "older adults" in the United States, which they defined as those between the ages of fifty-seven and eighty-five.

The premise was if doctors are going to help this older age-group keep sexuality in good shape, they have to know what is happening in the bedrooms. Researchers talked to more than three thousand men and women about a variety of intimate topics, including sexual history, masturbation practices, oral sex preference, sexually transmitted diseases, and so forth. Two further reports, one in the *New England Journal of Medicine* in August 2007 and an initial examination of sexual problems in the *Journal of Sexual Medicine* in September 2008, substantiated the 2004 findings of the sexual habits of older adults. As a result of this study, researchers began to see future sexual trends for seniors.

Because the boomer population is turning sixty, there is interest in how aging affects sexuality. And I am sure that the boomers, a group that created the context for the sexual revolution, is more than curious about developing an understanding of how their sex life is going to be affected at seventy-five. Nearly 40 percent of males between the ages of seventy-five and eighty-five are sexually active according to the National Social Life, Health, and Aging Project. It is less for women, only 17 percent. I don't know whether to be surprised at that statistic or not, but I certainly call that a healthy percentage. I've heard many stories about active libidos in nursing homes. My friend's eight-nine-year-old mother has a boyfriend in her geriatric community. These studies prove that the sexual shelf life is extending, and it seems in the near future that there may not be a definite expiration date on intimacy.

The following is a representative sampling of some surprising facts:

About 69 percent of men and 40 percent of women have engaged in some form of sexual activity with a partner, and these sexually active people have sex twice a month; nearly a quarter of these sexually active people have sex four times a month or more. Sex is still important to nearly two-thirds of women and 90 percent of the men; vaginal intercourse is the sexual activity of choice for most of the people most of the time. Oral sex is popular too, especially for more than half of both men and women in the "under seventy-five" crowd; about half the men and a quarter of women masturbate.

The actual aging process doesn't cause sexual problems. Problems are caused by difficulty in achieving orgasm (about 35 percent of the women) and simple lack of interest by women (45 percent) and erectile dysfunction (40 percent). There are lubrication problems, as well as stress and depression problems.

It is interesting to know that for both men and women, having a steady romantic partner strongly determines the quality of their sex life. However, women are less likely to be married or in an intimate relationship at any age. Yet, nearly eight in ten men have a steady partner, but only four in ten women do. As women age, the number may even be less.

I'm learning that the key to having sex with benefits is a happy, healthy and socially connected style of living that includes talking about sex. There are too many nuances, too many emotions ruminating in our minds at any age, let alone in our sixties, to adopt a casual attitude about the subject. For example, aging men have a tendency to become more like women in their approach to sex. They might need a little coaxing; or they may need to ask for more patience, cooperation, and skillful stimulation. Artfully negotiating sex through clear communication can achieve a very pleasant result. Speaking candidly and in a relaxed manner is crucial for a relationship to grow and develop. In any relationship where sex is involved, unbalanced sexual fulfillment is a prelude to an eventual parting of the ways.

One of my anecdotal references occurred when I dated the Sicilian for a year and became familiar with the sexual proclivities of a man over sixty. This man was wise to the ways of keeping up testosterone levels. I had no idea that a man could take shots to increase the male hormone levels or that there was a topical testosterone cream, which also assists in boosting the male sex drive. The Sicilian was in fantastic shape, and he even put me in better shape with a diet of more protein and less carbohydrates, with major doses of omega-3s. However, the real secret to successful intimacy with any man or woman is not just a good diet and plenty of exercise or even a man's sexual prowess. I'd rather make love to a great mind and a beautiful soul.

Recently, it was my pleasure to meet a younger man. Fully aware that I was older, he was not fazed by my age and more focused on my energy. If a woman has the opportunity in her sixties to date a younger man, she might consider it. Of course, that's all about the luck of the draw and whom you meet at Whole Foods. But when it happens, it's kind of a thrill to know that happiness and energy are an aphrodisiac. I'm also reminded that attraction is all about energy and not necessarily about the perfect body. I always try to stay away from thinking about how I appear to a man physically and focus on the Zen of the experience. That's the magic in attraction. That's when the world stops for a moment, and I am in the vortex of the Tao. In the end, I'm probably more comfortable with men closer to my age. On the other hand, see the text message from Annie above. His dick was amazing.

IT'S A VICIOUS RUMOR

Our modern society is obsessively focused on youth and the physical characteristics of a person. But not every sixty year-old man chases after a younger woman. And while it is fun to get attention from a younger man, the reality is that a sixty year-old woman is usually not going to hold the young man's attention for long. Any man or woman living in the present with full awareness of the positive aspects of living well with balanced energy and self-mastery will think twice about becoming a social cliché.

Boomers, just by sheer numbers, are the majority of the population in the country; and we are still sexy and vibrant. Falling prey to a youth culture is an undignified pastime. We are vibrant singular forces in the universe we created; we have the energy and the passion to carpe diem and seize not just the day, but also each moment in life, and we have the fortitude to select our thongs or boxers carefully. We do not need to throw the keys into a bowl and take potluck or let just anyone drive our cars. The sexual revolution is over, so let's choose our memories and our friends carefully in our sixties. It's a vicious rumor that we are not a commanding sexual presence in our society.

Which leads me to my last riff on wearing a thong.

THE TAO OF SEX TOYS

The word "masturbation," the art of pleasing oneself sexually, is still a red flag word in our English vernacular. People cringe, especially when a woman mentions the "M" word. It's downright shocking because it's just not done in polite society. You mean, a woman masturbates?

I recently took a stand-up comedy class at UCLA. While waiting for my turn to do my five-minute shtick on "Me and My Shadow," I decided to launch into a riff on "The only thing I hate more than eating alone is having sex alone." Embarrassed laughter filled the classroom. I wanted to see how freely expressive and funny I could be with the subject of masturbation. It's true: humor crosses all taboos.

One of the first taboos I remember as a Catholic adolescent, besides getting pregnant out of wedlock, was that masturbation was forbidden. The girls thought it was just a boy thing. No one told the girls that it was even a possibility. I guess the church didn't know girls could masturbate. I didn't even know what it was about until my late twenties. You mean a woman could pleasure herself without anyone else around? What a concept! I had one friend in Las Vegas who spoke about masturbation and her vibrator with great fondness. One day, it went off randomly and vibrated through the dresser drawer. I had never seen one before, let alone used one. When I was married, I rarely played around with that idea (no pun intended). I was too busy and/or not interested. I didn't even know if my ex was interested. It was literally years before I ever considered masturbation as a sexual option. I suppose when one doesn't start off as a masturbator, one's thoughts don't run on that track.

Men are masturbators. I don't know how many times a week a man masturbates, but the ones I have spoken to about this tell me that they masturbate every two to three days. One man said to me, "If you don't use it, you lose it." Makes sense to me. The penis is a muscle, and a muscle has to be used in order to function regularly. Women have muscles in the pelvic region, and I consider it important that these muscles are also used regularly. But that's where yoga becomes important as a practice for women and for men. Every posture in yoga uses the pelvic muscles. I want to consider a new mantra: let's use our sexual muscles for good and keep a healthy sensual sense of self.

My friend Annie was the culprit who refined my idea of the fine art of masturbation. Not only does she have a huge box of sex toys available at all times, but she also designs sex toys. She even had a twelve-inch robot that assists in masturbation, and this robot was scarier than a few men I have known. Who needs a man when a twelve-inch robot is available?

One day, I went through her sex toy box and examined the really sophisticated sex toys. Then Annie took me on a tour of sex toys on the Internet, and that's when I discovered there was an alternative sex universe. She asked me what I liked to use. I had one sort of banana-shaped dildo that was psychedelic blue that the Sicilian gave me, but I rarely used it. The batteries finally rusted, and I threw it out.

"You never used it because it's boring," Annie said to me one day.

Annie grabbed one sex toy after another from her toy box. She took me into the freezer section of her refrigerator and showed me clay molds of penises that she had planned to make into sex toys. The woman was a mechanical genius! I was living the Tao of sex toys!

INT. ANNIE'S KITCHEN - NIGHT
JOAN and ANNIE are staring at the clay penis molds in the refrigerator.

                      ANNIE
Want to take one home?

                      JOAN
What am I going to do with it?
They're not hard yet.

Annie turns to the box of sex

toys on the kitchen table. She pulls out a robot.

          ANNIE
How about this?

          JOAN
That's intimidating, and I've got a lot of Catholic guilt and shame left over.

          ANNIE
They'll always be here if you want one. By the way, what do you use besides an old-fashioned dildo?

          JOAN
My middle finger?

          ANNIE
That's boring and uncreative. Sex should be fun.

          JOAN
I know, but it gets the job done.

What has surprised me during the anecdotal research of *60, Sex & Tango* has been the inherent interest by both men and women about the importance of discussing sex. Whenever I go out with my male and female friends or male friends with benefits, we inevitably discuss sexual issues between men and women. The conversation starts off with a little tension, one or both may be ill at ease; but several sentences into the discussion, the dialogue becomes an energetic and fascinating study of how men and women relate to sex and how sexual needs can be met, especially the sexual needs of women over sixty.

Males and females are not so different in how they think about sex. They are more similar in their needs and desires than one would imagine. Not only does sex make for good conversation, but it also brings the taboo subject of sex into the mainstream.

The Tao of sex is still alive and well among the boomers. It's just that the sexual revolution we once knew has taken on a new perspective.

Text message from Peter
darling, busy can't do Sat. night
it's the Italians
wanted u to know asap
loathe this form of communication
i adore u precious angel

CHAPTER 9
WHEN YOUR BEST FRIEND IS NOT YOUR LOVER

It's lovely to be in love, but sometimes it can be stranger than fiction. Love can often be painful and often stifling. While being in love, life often stands still, and there is no movement or growth. On the other hand, being in love can be inspirational and uplifting as the heart soars. Love is not always constant or easy. As we get older, the concept of what love is may even be redefined as life's circumstances change, or as married couples realize that their individual needs not being met.

For boomer couples that are married, perhaps romantic love cooled off years ago. By the time the children finished college, left home, got married, and started raising their own family, the husband and perhaps the wife were winding down their respective careers. If the wife was not working, she had to contend with the husband being home most of the time or stood by while he took up golf with a vengeance. She was resentful; he was resentful that she was resentful. Clearly, they were seeing too much of each other. She decided she wanted her freedom back; he decided he wanted to build a consulting practice. The marriage was stale, even dysfunctional. Worse, they weren't talking to each other.

Why do some couples feel surrounded by a void of loneliness in the midst of a marriage with a partner who has not only been the most important person in his or her life, but also has been a best friend for forty years or more?

I have many friends who are married. Some women and men express to me that they feel a longing for some kind of freedom that expresses itself in further individuation. Wanderlust sets in; daydreams fill up the alone time and distractions are commonplace. She wants her sex life back. He wants his freedom back. The marriage just feels distinctly uncomfortable and wrong.

I have ruminated from time to time about what people in long-term relationships might do to stimulate creativity and/or generate excitement while living in a peaceful environment. David and I were together for almost sixteen years, and I was married for eighteen years. I have some experience being a part of a couple. The fact that I am not married now and that my chance at another long-term relationship may be slim to none does not make me immune to the problems couples face. I will always search for harmonious expression whether I am single or in a committed "we" relationship.

Creative or harmonic expressions are difficult to actualize when daily irritations hold center stage in relationships. There is a laundry list of dissatisfactions with our mates' habits, proclivities, or behavior that might be unacceptable when it is viewed under a microscope of daily activity. Closeness fosters dependence; sometimes it can be the husband who gets more dependent on his wife and not the other way around. Perhaps, one person in the dyad may take better care of himself or herself. "You look great," a wife says to her husband. "And I look fat." There may too much neediness and not enough separation on the part of both partners. My married friends tell me that sex is infrequent or nonexistent; even intimacy is rare. Where did all the excitement go?

The reality is that a man, married or single, will probably wake up one day and wonder why he has three houses, a plane, a penthouse on the Las Vegas Strip that he overpaid for, undervalued stock options, some margin calls, and a 401(k) worth less than when he started to save for retirement. His wife or partner nags him about the vacation home in Cabo that he shares with his cousin because she wants to explore exotic places around the world, like go on a safari in Kenya for the bargain price of $15,000 apiece or to the Osho Ashram in Pune, India, where she can meditate for a week and where they can both take classes in self-mastery. But he holds three mortgages, the housing market is sinking, and he can't afford to trade any of his assets for a life of more free time. He has no breathing room left. He is sick and tired of playing golf out of habit on Sunday morning; she is sick and tired of spending half of her Sunday watching Meet the Press while she waits to do something fun with her husband or partner like going to a movie or to the zoo or to the Getty for a picnic or go for a drive up the coast to Santa Barbara to the Montecito Inn. For God's sake, does it take that long to play eighteen holes? "Is he drinking a beer with his buddies at the club bar instead of having lunch with me?" she asks as she leaves the house to go shopping. As a woman discerns a lack of interest in her needs or desires or both, she fantasizes about taking a Latin lover and getting all her health benefits covered. Or, the wife simply decides to leave her husband and her marriage and go off to live in their unrented condo.

GET A WRECKING CREW AND CLEAN UP THIS MESS

To state the obvious, just thinking about being married forty years can be exhausting. We tell and retell our life stories over and over again to each other; and these stories are merely shadows of who we are, manifesting themselves as life's illusions. In psychological terms, the shadow is that part of the psyche that is hidden, obscuring our aspirations, our virtues, and our ability to see clearly without shame and guilt.

Who is really our wife? Who is really our husband? Do we really know the sentient being who is our mate? I think it is not possible to know another human being completely. There is just too much exterior distraction that gets in the way of knowing, understanding, and empathizing with a mate. The easy path is to continue the addiction to externals (i.e., TV and hobbies) and hide behind the façade of a couple and continue the complacency. However, just because there are no surprises anymore and little mystery left in the relationship, it does not mean that a couple cannot reconnect themselves emotionally to each other. It takes a concerted effort and perseverance to continue on the path of love.

GET OUT OF YOUR CAVE AND FIND SOME LIGHT, DUDE

When questions come up in conversation about why there is a discontent in a marriage of forty years or more, I don't have specific answers because I am not intimately involved in the day-to-day activities of a married couple whose marriage has gone stale after the children have left; but I have a few observations.

I suspect that the health of a long-term relationship requires both parties to accept that the living situation is in flux and has produced a new dynamic. Add to this mix a conscious or unconscious awareness on the part of both spouses that there is a need for individual growth and transformation especially in the later decades of life. When neither interests nor compatibility hold the couple together anymore, the "we" is lacking a spiritual, deeper connection. The "we" has lost its collective mind. It's time to think outside the box and create new ways to become intimate. However, whatever the new dynamic turns out to be, if the couple decides to redefine their loving relationship, both partners will have to engage in a conscious commitment and a determined willingness to stay together.

Of course, it is easier to sweep problems under the rug or play the blame game because talking about the many changes occurring within the collective marriage mind is complicated and exhausting. Anyway, is the other spouse really even listening? And what's the point of all the dialogue if the old dog can't learn new tricks?

One of the ways to open up discussions about the changing dynamics in a marriage is to challenge the status of the collective marriage mind by seeking therapy. After all, if the couple has endured a marriage for forty years or more, it might be worth exploring the on-going relationship on the unconscious level rather than discussing the relationship on the basis of material possessions. A commitment to therapy necessitates bravery, fearlessness, and the ability to set the ego aside. Granted, that's a pretty big task for anyone, no matter the age, but the opportunity to gain insight into marriage as a collective identity and to reinvigorate the enthusiasm of identifying as a couple is a valuable tool for creating happiness.

Shaikh Abu-Said Abil-Kheir, one of the earlier Sufi poets who lived more than two centuries before Rumi, the most famous Sufi poet in history, offers good advice to men and women in a relationship or even not in a relationship:

"Take one step away from yourself—and behold!—the path!"

I suspect that ritual and habit are only two of the deadly killers of spontaneity and creativity in a marriage or partnership. Ego is the third and most potent killer. Put the ego mind aside if you want a good marriage or relationship.

I've seen unhappiness in the eyes of my married friends and partners. I've heard voices raised in frustration and anger and asked myself, "Where is the caring tone, the effort to comfort, the cherishing nature, the sweetness that was once upon a time part of their relationship?" Someone does not always have to be right in an argument. "I know what I'm talking about. You don't know anything about anything." These arguments can go on for weeks. Or sometimes couples feel more comfortable just not talking to each other, staying in the safe zone of nonconfrontation as silence fills every room of their perfectly decorated five-thousand-square-foot house.

No one said it was going to be easy to stay committed for decades. Does anyone even remember his or her marriage vows?

Years ago, I had the illusion that my significant other was going to complete my being and be my soul mate for life. I got over it in my sixties. That might happen at the beginning of a relationship when love is all we need, but the reality is that each person in the dyad is just trying to hang on and maintain some sense of self. I remember hanging on to my relationship with David. We were loath to confront anything other than what was on the surface because, really, why put strains on our relationship after all the years of togetherness? Why bring unpleasant memories out in the open and scratch old wounds that provoke conflict?

There has to be some hope somewhere in a relationship; otherwise, one or the other or both members of the dyad will end up being a nasty pessimist and a miserable human being. I know men and women who have had enough pain and misery with their spouse and finally left the marriage without the benefit of a therapist or couple's marriage counseling. In one instance, I personally know of a wife who left her husband after forty-five years of marriage because her husband had too much energy for his own passions, and she felt left out of the marriage. She couldn't compete with the energy and enthusiasm he expended toward his other interests; she felt it was time to explore life on her own terms. In another case, the husband could not endure another moment of boring, ritualized sameness and a lack of concern for the other. Plus, the wife refused to shop or cook anymore. The husband told me, "One more moment of togetherness, and I'm going to have a nervous breakdown."

I'm looking for the million-dollar answer that counteracts the lethargy in marriage so that love will not die of attrition when rituals change, when effective communication no longer exists, or when physical passion dies. I want to believe in a new relationship paradigm that bridges conflicting forces of energy and solidifies the bonds of shared values: children, grandchildren, and a commonality of goals.

I don't necessarily need a physical focus in a relationship anymore; I am searching for a spiritual core that interfaces devotion and friendship. The recognition that mates are fellow travelers on a shared voyage is a reflection that we are the agents of growth and change. It means that together and separately, couples can perpetuate the ideal of consistent love without giving up our sense of self.

I heard a story the other day about an Israeli couple in their midforties. They have five children, and both of them work. They live simply but are able to provide sufficiently for their family. When they work, they work hard. When they play, they play together. They make love twice a day every day. They dance together with joy.

They make time to be alone with each other and talk to each other about their interests and passions. They do not use the children as a wedge to separate themselves from each other. Their love is complete and joyous.

They are beholding the path!

IT HURTS SO GOOD

Being alone is no picnic either. Since I've been on both sides, I can guarantee that singles also have daily challenges. Sometimes I can often go several weeks without a meaningful conversation with another person. Some people might think that would be the perfect existence. More often than not, I miss the excitement and devotion provided by intellectual and emotional connection. Single people seem to become bored easily because they have no one to share intimacies with or to banter with. Sometimes singles become cranky and mean and reluctant to engage with the outside world. Single people have a tendency to watch a lot of television or use the Internet excessively. Mindless activity provokes no creative thinking. Who wants to read Thomas Friedman's *Hot, Flat, and Crowded* when you can watch *Dancing with the Stars?* I'm not a big fan of receiving a slew of jokes on e-mails sent to a list of people I don't know. It's numbing on the receiving end and unproductive on the sender's end. All right, once in a while, I get a really great YouTube video suggestion, but enough is enough!

I talk to myself from time to time, walking to my classes or shopping in the grocery store. I think I'm going mad, and I'm painfully embarrassed when someone hears me. Overusing the telephone is another idiosyncrasy of being single. Does that mean I'm bored, or I just like to talk? Both are signs of lapsing into an unconsciousness state that might better be replaced with contemplation.

My therapist, Mike, says that there is no such condition as boredom. Boredom is a state of mind that has its roots in inner discontent and not the lack of outward stimulation. Mike says stop talking out loud, overusing the tools of distraction, and free the mind through contemplation and mediation, which frees the mind by disengaging from thoughts so that a person can get to know the inner workings of the soul and thereby achieve self-mastery.

As a single woman, I have one overriding conundrum that married people do not experience. I usually feel at a loss when asked if my happiness is dependent on finding a companion or even getting married. Or am I truly content within myself? Am I enough for my own happiness? And can I be complete without a man?

I have trouble being honest with this question. I protest that I am not really looking for a man to be my long-term partner. I walk around my burg and think, "I'm not looking"; and to prove it, I walk with my head down, studying my flip-flops so I won't trip on the potholes in the road as I cross the street to Starbucks. Honest answer: I'm looking, folks, even though it makes me feel better to say I'm not looking. What's even crazier, I'm still looking despite my stranger-than-fiction odyssey dating on the Internet, separating from David, falling in love with Ben, going through several tryouts with a few new men to see if there was compatibility—all the while feeling an aching loss of David's presence. Yet, I reluctantly still want to couple even though there is enough testosterone in my family with two sons and four grandsons to fill up an all-boys' boarding school.

And now Aaron and Alyse are expecting another child. We have all agreed we do not want to know the sex of the baby. Although another grandson would be a joyous gift, a baby girl would be very sweet.

BLOODY ENGLISH

Throughout these last five years, I have had a best friend who is perfectly heterosexual and married. Peter is not and has never been my lover. The truth is that Peter is a perfect fit for me as a companion—with one exception. He is British and considers himself Lord of the Manor, which doesn't wash well with me at this age. Nonetheless, love is an accommodation. We speak to each other every day because of our need to connect. Ours is not a physical relationship, but our attraction has a combination of spiritual connection and physical energy that works well for both of us. We have clear boundaries with each other, and they are never crossed.

How lucky, how grateful I feel that this fully conscious man cherishes me, respects my abundant energy, and puts up with the crazy quilt of my life. He tempers his fondness for me with self-mastery and compassion. I am mystified at the way I handle this situation. Through it all, I am never jealous or grasping or cynical or sad. Our friendship is individuated on the basis of giving each other space and time. Since this is a meaningful relationship without physical attachment, Peter and I therefore, have no expectations or illusions about each other or our relationship. We simply share respect and devotion.

Peter is also my tango student. He insists on having a tango lesson with me once a week. I switch hats for an hour a week and work with him on his tango lead. He is a diligent student, and I am like a military drill sergeant. We have to balance the student-teacher relationship with the personal friendship, and it is often challenging. It's a whirlwind hour of intimate conversation mixed with some of the most thrilling tango music ever written. We religiously give each other this weekly hour of connection; then we try to put it all together afterward at a Mexican restaurant where I drink a margarita and he orders a pretentious British aperitif. When we can, we carry that energy through to the next night with sushi and our Saturday night *milonga*.

The universe dropped Peter into my life seven years ago without apology. I am devoted to him as my friend, but he is not my lover.

A BIRD IN THE HAND

Sometimes life throws you a curveball with a friend who is not your lover. When boundaries are crossed and friendship enters into the territory of the "becoming lovers" stage, there is a moment at which the friendship is in jeopardy. If the line is crossed, there is no turning back. Friendship may die.

Just recently, an old friend from the UCLA and Berkeley days had renewed our friendship. He was part of our Jewish gang back in the Berkeley law school days in the early 1960s. When I transferred to Berkeley in January of 1963, I met Levi (code name). He was funny and cute and kind of a wild guy. I loved to hang out with him;

but I only had eyes for my ex, who was serious, intellectual, and had more of that beatnik élan.

I heard he was in Los Angles teaching law at a local university for a semester, and I thought it would be fun to e-mail him. Although he had already returned back East to his home, he was certainly excited that I walked back into his life.

I had heard he was otherwise involved with a lady, and he quickly denied the rumor. But I was only looking for a kibitz, a latte, some newsy conversation; and I didn't want to interfere with anything he had going on.

"Don't fall in love before I get to LA," he said on the very first conversation. "I've always had a crush on you."

Here was my mistake: for three months, I thought Levi and I were deepening our friendship; and all the while, he was romancing me, and I was unconsciously flirting with him. I knew Levi was coming to Los Angeles in September to give a lecture, but he wanted to see me before September. So, I went through periods of being excited that there was possibly more to our friendship because we've all heard stories about people who have known each other in the past and get together later on in life because it's meant to be. But something wasn't adding up.

Intuition kicked in. In yoga, it's the sixth chakra, the third eye; and it sits between the brows. I don't always listen to it, but it functions quite well when I am fully conscious of that very powerful energy center. I always know when something is going to happen before it happens even though I don't have all the details worked out. Of course, it makes sense to be suspicious when the other person stops calling.

I found out Levi really had a girlfriend back East. She found out about me through a mutual friend. Levi's cover was blown. "I'm not in love with her. She's great, but we just date; we're good friends," he protested.

Then Levi went right on telling me we'd meet in Los Angeles very soon. Then silence again. More silence. I wrote to him, "What happened to you?"

E-MAIL FROM LEVI:
I was thinking about us. I have been somewhat disingenuous to both you and the woman I'm seeing. I'm not comfortable as this kind of situation is stressful and could cause cancer. I think it's best to postpone further contact so I still have your friendship and respect.

Levi wanted to get physical and then didn't want to get physical. Although we admitted our previous attraction, which generated intensity and energy on the phone, when guilt kicked in, he realized he was confused; and it frightened him. After all, he already had a girlfriend—a bird in the hand. He wanted forgiveness for crossing the line with me. I understood, but I couldn't go back to the bantering friendship we once had after acknowledging our virtual physical attraction even though we never acted on it. It was the thought that counted.

I take partial responsibility for the demise of our friendship. I needed to stay friends with boundaries and not get lost in the drama. Lesson learned. Keep your sixth chakra well oiled. The third eye comes in handy when there is deception waiting in the wings. I went to my refrigerator after getting Levi's e-mail and read one of my Buddhist sayings:

Do you have the patience to wait till your mud settles and the water is clear? Can you remain unmoving till the right action arises by itself?

—Tao Te Ching

I am always stunned by the profoundness in Tao Te Ching's questions. I can read it daily and almost despair at my answer. Can I wait, have patience, follow my own counsel, and remain unmoving till the right action arises by itself, without force, without pushing? I don't know. I am still in the process of finding the answer.

OLDIES BUT NOT GOODIES

It is truly amazing how I am continually learning new things at sixty-four. I was giving a yoga session to a private client this morning and was overcome by what I have said to myself over and over again: There is no script for living in our sixties. We're making it up as we go along, and there are so many surprises that it shakes me to the core sometimes. Who are friends? Who are lovers? Who are both?

Let's take the reverse on this "friends/lovers" theme. How long does it take for lovers to become just friends? Is it actually possible? There are so many different twists and variations on this theme; for example, David and I remained good friends after we separated. Over twenty years ago, the theater director and I were once a couple and lived together, and we are now the best of friends. In both cases, time was on our side for healing and personal growth. This is the beauty of forgiveness and openness.

And then there is Ben. He came back into my life last night. It was unexpected, but not so surprising. I had sent him a birthday e-mail a few days before. I wanted to know if we were still friends, if we indeed had created a balance between intimacy and friendship.

Several days later, Ben e-mailed me a short film that he knew I would love. I thanked him for sending it. Later that evening, he called. The ice had been broken. I saw his number come up on the phone and was curious about how I was going to feel about him, what emotions would come up after seven months of no contact.

I answered the phone calmly. We caught up on family and professional projects like we always used to do after a long hiatus. He was in Santa Monica, and he wanted to talk about the book I was writing.

"I know about publishing," he said with confidence. "Want to talk on the phone, or do you want me to come over?"

"Come over," I said calmly. It was time to face my demon.

INT. JOAN'S APARTMENT - NIGHT
BEN enters JOAN's apartment. Ben looks around as if it was for the first time.

                    BEN
          Those paintings ... they're new?

                    JOAN
          No. Everything is the same.

                    BEN
          What is it then?

                    JOAN
          I painted the wall.

                    BEN
          It's great. It changes everything. Can I have some water? I'm dying of thirst.

Ben takes off his jacket and sits on the couch. He is uncomfortable.

Joan brings him the water. It is an awkward moment.

                    BEN
          I've been keeping myself in good shape. How do I look?

                    JOAN
          You look good. It's been seven months.

> BEN
> Well, my partner got sick after we finished the documentary, and I've been taking care of my folks.

> JOAN
> I'm a grandmother again. Another boy.

> BEN
> My son had another girl. Three girls.

We were not strangers because we were familiar with the details of our lives. We had been lovers and then not lovers, and from the beginning, we were friends who shared our lives. I wanted to discover if there was anything left of our friendship.

How many skins had I shed in those seven months? How much time had I put into coming out of the cave to see light instead of living with shadows so I could know myself? How much had I changed?

Somewhere in the middle of the conversation on the couch, with a pillow between us, the unspoken subtext became louder and clearer than the spoken words. I knew I had been completely in love with Ben; but I felt that Ben could only love me in increments, sporadically, and that was all he was capable of doing. He didn't even know why he couldn't love me enough to embrace my love because he seemed as full of confusion as ever. His heart was closed to the full spectrum of love.

I wasn't sad or angry or flustered about this state of being. I was simply present and responsive and finally ready to surrender. Mike said that no man is complete without the ability to love a woman. Ben might never be complete.

An hour went by; then Ben got up to leave. Although we had talked about many subjects, I wasn't sure if Ben had connected with me in that hour. He put on his jacket slowly. In the past, when Ben started to leave, he stalled by looking for his keys or glasses; then the energy in the room became sexually charged. We finally had no familiar narrative story to play out. Ben hugged me and held me close. He kissed me quickly on the lips before he let go. When he opened the door to leave, he asked me if I still got the *Los Angeles Times* delivered in the morning. He used to throw it back inside the room when he left at dawn. The ritual had ended.

Will I ever know anything about men? Men are a mystery—like love, like how the heart works, like my passion for dancing tango. The only truth I consistently recognize is that I wake up every day with gratitude and with the intention to go through life with an open heart and a true sense of forgiveness. I vow to live light and carry only what I need. And I cherish my beautiful family and my honest, beloved friends.

When balance returns to my wounded heart, I repeat the offering of Lao Tzu, the sixth-century father of Taoism and a Chinese philosopher:

The practice of the Tao consists in daily losing.

THE MALE MYSTIQUE

Men sometimes say they don't understand women. Men and women have different natures, perspectives and needs. Women are considered a complicated gender because they have different nuances in their psychological makeup.

The one true common denominator among women is that they are born to bond, to nurture, to listen and to empathize. Women are touchy-feely creatures who delight in familiar female responses. Women also have a more acute sense of intuition. When a woman's best male friend is not her lover, her level of interest reflects a friendship parity that is consistent with her relationships with female friends. Since chemistry does not exist in the equation, the friendship has less emotional complications.

Just recently, one of my students told me that her best guy friend expressed deeper feelings toward her. He was convinced they would end up married. My student had no previous warning that this was in his mind, and she was mystified.

Previously, there had been full disclosure, no expectations and no emotional complications. But she knew too much about her friend—specifically, that he was unable to stay with a woman for any length of time. She also noticed that he took shortcuts in his pursuit of gaining her love. He glossed over salient points of their long friendship and seemed unconcerned with her negative response to his entreaties because in his mind, they were going to be together eventually. Crossing the divide from friendship to lover was too large a leap for my student. But the man saw it as a natural progression of their friendship.

With men, I sometimes feel that the old saying of "What you see is what you get" is actually a cover for laziness or lack of focus. Because men like to keep things simple in life, they often prefer to respond to situations and people in a less adroit manner because coming up with a deeper, more honest response is difficult and challenging. Men cannot take too much information coming at them quickly, so they sometimes won't engage or are just plain disingenuous. It is easier to lie or evade.

Mendacity in men is frustrating. I'm not implying that women are never disingenuous or that women are not capable of dissembling. Men have a hard time figuring out women too. However, women want to believe what a man is telling them is the absolute truth. It is always shocking when a woman figures out that her boyfriend has another woman on the side or another family in Detroit or likes to go to gay bars on the weekends or use the Internet for his porn addiction. And then because of recent news stories about cheating celebrities, the question of whether men are hardwired for multiple sex partners really puts women on the defensive.

I have been truly frustrated by the lack of full disclosure with the men I have known; so I am upfront about the need to be clear, forthright, and truthful when talking to a man.

"There is nothing to be afraid of, darling," I say sweetly to the man.

However, in the end, when all is said and done, we are all just guessing about human behavior between the sexes. Recently, I met a woman I know in the bank who told me innocently that a man I was dating had hit on her and her friend at an eating establishment. This dating companion of mine was obviously still looking for love in all the wrong places. In essence, we are who we are.

WHERE, O WHERE HAVE ALL THE FLOWERS GONE?

In this moment, I am completely joyful to have my women yoginis as my beloved friends. We share the bliss of yoga and give each other many gifts: support, love, compassion and time. We grieve at each other's sadness; we laugh at each other's joys. We are mostly traveling in different directions because we are of all ages, from twenty-eight to sixty-eight; but age is unimportant because our connection is spiritual, and our paths are all divine. We all live with consciousness and patience. We are kindred spirits, deeply forgiving to one another because of our mutual respect and honor. This is the essence of an enduring and constant friendship.

My friend Corinne said to me one day when I was feeling a little down about being alone, "Check out the good things, J. You don't have to curl your eyelashes anymore because they're growing with our new favorite product, Revitalash. You're having a good hair day. You're eyes aren't red and burning because we don't have the Santa Ana winds. You don't have a dry vagina; you've got a good sex drive, a friend with benefits, and good sunspot coverage. What more is there?"

I postulate friendship and love are one in the same. When your best friend is not your lover, your best friend is your lover in a deeper spiritual sense. In my sixties, I began to make small changes in my life regarding whom I wanted to spend my time with, where I wanted to put my energy, and what brings me joy. These intentions required altering a few priorities and not resisting changes that I must make in order to follow my bliss so I won't run the risk of coming up empty in my seventies. If I keep digging in my past archives for soulful sustenance making reference to people, places, and things that once created a life in another time, I will probably not be able to experience the present with clarity. I will stay in the cave and only see shadows. I will languish without light and love. Friendship is more about deepening an abiding love that centers on devotion and trust between two people.

This is a gift I give myself. It is also a gift that brings joy to others.

PART 3
TANGO

A phone call from David's daughter Camille
Dad died

CHAPTER 10
HE DID IT HIS WAY

Life threw me for a loop. I was in the beginning stages of writing about awareness, about mindfulness, about moving forward in my life, about finding a graceful way to grow old, about finding some inner peace. Chapter 1 was finished, and the phone rang. I looked at the number, and I knew it was Camille, David's daughter.

And I knew why she was calling. I knew that David—her father, my soul mate—had died. His death did not come as a shock because he was on his final journey, the next transition of many incarnations. He was inevitably going to die of liver failure. Prospects looked dim for a liver transplant at UCLA. He was hanging on to life as tenaciously as he had lived.

I had just put on Sinatra. I poured a glass of wine before making dinner. David loved Sinatra and would listen to him endlessly. There is a vocal note that Sinatra sings that resonates in my body and brings me into David's soul. I cannot explain that sound, but when I hear it, my heart beats faster.

"My Funny Valentine" was playing. I was going to call David the next day. We continue our dance, our tango, even though we separated, even though he was sick. The music made me happy and sad at the same time.

"Don't change a hair for me, not if you care for me ... each day is Valentine's Day."

David was larger than life, the overriding love of my life for sixteen years and thereafter; and forever after, he will be "my summertime, my wintertime ..." In the moment of recognition of his death, I knew the void would never be filled. Our souls had met, and our hearts had opened to love and joy.

Fairy tales can come true,
it can happen to you,
if you're young at heart.
For it's hard you will find
to be narrow of mind,
if you're young at heart.
You can go to extremes
with impossible schemes,
You can laugh when your dreams
fall apart at the seams.

And life gets more exciting
with each passing day,
And love is either in your heart
or on its way.
Don't you know that's worth
every treasure on earth,
To be young at heart.
For as rich as you are
it's much better by far
To be young at heart.

And if you should survive to 105,
look at all you'll derive
out of being alive.
And here is the best part
you have head start,
If you are among the very
Young at heart.

David Garcia, 1941–2008

Text message from myself to myself
never thought I'd b alone at 64
not what I wanted
so make the best of it
accept w joy & gratitude

CHAPTER 11
BEING ALONE: IT HURTS SO GOOD

I used to think that living alone for the rest of my life was going to be the worst thing that could befall me. The idea of aloneness was disturbing and often frightening. I don't know exactly how long it took me to overcome my fear of living alone. Maybe it was many years, maybe it was yesterday, maybe I'm still afraid.

Previously, and sometimes now intermittently, I felt that being alone was causing an ever-increasing rise in my stress levels. I even had persistent heartburn. There were no contrasts in my life. If my life were a canvas, it would be the color gray. I was often tired, but never lethargic. I entertained retiring, but from what? Life? Retirement was a terrifying thought, like facing certain death. Or was I going to succumb to the ties that bind and move to Las Vegas with the prospects of becoming an on-call babysitter to my grandsons? What was going to happen to my personal life? Would I ever fall in love again, or would any man have the courage to love me again after David swept me off my feet? And then there were those terrifying moments when I felt I never wanted to write or dance again.

Then without warning, I began to step outside myself and see myself as a sentient and conscious being. It happened when I was meditating. It was a fleeting moment. I was distancing myself from myself, which produced a state of detachment about who I am in the present and what I was able to control and not control. As a result, I was able to cultivate some clear emotions regarding who I am, what I want, and where I was going. I wasn't judging or labeling my emotions; rather, I was watching my emotions, just sitting with them. In that conscious state, I was able to set aside the unconscious illusions (more like delusions) that usually float inside my mind. By stepping outside myself, I was beginning to put one foot in front of the other and walk my unique path with mindfulness.

Then one day, without warning, out of the blue on a Sunday, I didn't need to call a guy friend to help me get through the seventh day of the week. I could actually live by myself without sharing the dreaded Sunday with another human being. Sunday, bloody Sunday, was gone. I was over being alone.

HELL'S KITCHEN

However, I'm never quite over being alone because the two things that I intensely dislike doing alone are cooking and having solitary sex. Cooking and sex are creative activities and meant to be shared with another person.

I confess that I'm not an eater. Food is there to keep me alive. Don't hate me and do not pity me. I was even a lousy eater as a child. My mother, a home economics major in college, made me eat everything on my plate. Every meal was nutritious but bland. She didn't believe in salt, let alone pepper. We were never allowed junk food, which meant I had to sneak a Coke and French fries at the local hangout after school. At dinner, I cleverly stashed the food in a napkin or got rid of it by feeding it to my fat dog or dumping it in the garbage as I cleared the table. I was so devious that I even put some of my food on my brother's plate. My mother was obsessed with having all of us eat everything on our plate, especially the vegetables. It was all nutritious and completely tasteless.

On the other hand, I had cooked for my family for so many years—having made thousands of breakfasts, lunches, and dinners for my children—that the thought of continuing to cook for myself for the duration of my life was unthinkable.

Today, Whole Foods is my main source of sustenance. Without Whole Foods a block away, I would be shrinking into near death from starvation. And I have to eat to work because what I do every day would kill a dray horse. After teaching classes all day, I'm physically and mentally exhausted. The thought of cooking is an anathema.

I have a terrible habit of standing and eating at the kitchen counter while reading the remains of the recently pared-down/abbreviated version of the *Los Angeles Times*, a once vibrant and richly reported metropolitan newspaper that hardly carries journalist status anymore. I know it's not good to eat standing up just as I know that reading the *Times* is a waste of time (no pun intended), but old habits die hard. I clean up the dishes and go back to my computer to write. The evening is just about over for me at nine o'clock because I need the sleep. I wake up at six in the morning to National Public Radio. This is my celebration of Groundhog Day.

SEPARATE TABLES
I feel quite different about eating when I have company. For someone who looks like she needs a sandwich, I do like to cook on occasion for a special friend. It gives me an outlet for creativity in the kitchen. My children tease me that I'm not a good cook; but I make a great brisket, a heck of a good roasted chicken, chili, and homemade soup. I love vegetables and salads and take pride in their preparation. But when I dine out, food tastes better, the atmosphere gives off mouth-watering aromas, and conversation creates excitement and encourages food consumption.

But I cannot eat out alone. I loathe sitting at a table by myself. David loved eating alone at restaurants, and he would tease me unmercifully about missing out on the joys of single dining. I cannot think of anything more terrifying than that. Everyone would be looking at me sitting at a table alone. "Who's that lonely spinster sitting by herself? Poor thing. She must be readying herself to commit suicide by taking her last meal alone with a good glass of Argentine red wine."

However, when I'm in Europe or Buenos Aires eating alone in a restaurant, I don't feel self-conscious. The atmosphere is cosmopolitan coupled with an element of mystery. The first time I ate alone was in Paris on the Left Bank. I was fifty-nine years old. During the day, I would walk through two or three arrondissements and dance tango at night along the quay (the Seine River). The first night I was alone without my friend, I walked happily along the streets near the Sorbonne where I was living (in a garret, of course reliving my youth) and looked inside the little cafes and bars to visualize myself inside. I selected a Lebanese restaurant. It was small and cozy; and more to the point, they did not serve French food, which I loathe. It turned out the owners were from Los Angeles. Of course! I took a seat in the corner and looked around. It wasn't entirely full yet. I studied my menu; and within a few minutes, I looked up, and the place was packed. And everyone decided to light up a cigarette at the same time! I choked down my food and left the restaurant in a hurry. It was so very French.

Paradoxically, while I loathe the idea of eating alone in restaurants, I am intrigued by the potential romance surrounding dining alone.

I'm a woman of questionable disrepute in a 1940s black-and-white film. I am dressed in a stylish tight-fitting gray tailored suit with a stand-up white collar, wearing a chic black hat that sits gingerly at a tilt on my head. Dark curls tumble down around my long neck.

I take off my white gloves with a dainty flick of the wrist and set them down on the table by my menu. I draw my ungloved hand to my hair to make sure there are no misplaced strands. I smell the exquisite red rosebud in a simple white china vase on the table. Then I look around the room in fascination and view a room full of people conversing in low tones through clouds of swirling smoke. I study the men who talk to each other and watch their wives making polite comments to one another about their jewelry or their new taffeta dresses with yards of shimmering flounce. An obsequious older waiter approaches the table and gestures with a slight bow. I order a simple salad with mushrooms, a fromage quiche, and a glass of dry red French table wine. This is done rapidly and without extraneous conversation.

An attractive middle-aged man with a pencil-thin mustache, wearing an elegant pin-striped black suit, stares at me from across the room. Do I know him? I might. Maybe we met at the art gallery opening in

Lower Manhattan last weekend. I smile demurely back and look down at my gloves, fondling them with charming femininity. I am alone, but I am happy. At this moment, one is not the loneliest number.

One may not be the loneliest number in my movie, but one is still the loneliest number in my kitchen.

THE PLEASURE CHEST

No matter the decade, I don't think that I will ever exhaust the topic of sex. And, since I am single, I am continually confronted with the stark reality that I am the person solely responsible for creating my own sexual pleasure.

I keep telling myself that it is perfectly normal for anyone at any age to engage in pleasurable sexual experiences and fantasies, even a single woman in her sixties. It's completely disingenuous to deny this aspect of our nature. After all, sex is ubiquitous in Western society. Everywhere we look—in magazines, store windows, on TV—it's the selling of sex. I pass a store called Bebe every morning on my drive to UCLA. The front of the store takes up a quarter of a block, and the window display looks like an advertisement for a bordello that specializes in bondage. The display always reminds me of the book I once wrote about two women who one-upped one another with their sexual fantasies. The women wore similar apparel.

The world of yoga is not immune from sexual discussions. Before, during, and after yoga, my friends and I have ongoing conversations about how Daniel Craig is the sexiest man on the planet and who wouldn't want to spend a night with him. I've also heard numerous male sexual fantasies along the way.

However, the subject of masturbation never comes up in the polite society. I'm not sure if everyone on the planet masturbates; yet, I am comfortable thinking that single people masturbate, unless committed to celibacy, because the opposite sex or even the same sex is not present to satisfy sexual needs

I let my imagination run amok when I am alone and thinking about sex. It might involve a random meeting with a strange man or someone I have a crush on, or my fantasy might involve a movie scenario where danger lurks in the alleys of Venice. And the danger turns into a sexual encounter. What about a threesome? Erica Jong's book *Fear of Flying* is always good for a fantasy scenario. I like the idea of sexual fantasies when I'm in the mood; however, sex toys are too plastic for my taste. They can be useful if you close your eyes and imagine the toy is, well, actually a real man or woman. And then there are the Penthouse letters to the editor, which may excite the mind and lead one to a better-than-average orgasm.

Sexual fantasies open up the mind and stimulate the pleasure area of our brain, creating opportunities for more sexual creativity. Fantasies are liberating; however, as I point out in my novel Women Obsessed, living out sexual fantasies in the real world can cause great emotional and psychic damage.

THE WAY WE WERE

Living alone prompts some really bad habits. One habit I have is a propensity to chase the past in order to avoid the present. When that does not work, I fantasize about a fabricated, unrealistic future that I think will make my world better. Big mistake. I do this kind of thinking less and less now, probably because the movies I play in my head produce dead ends. When I look at old scrapbooks and ruminate over memories or play the old tapes in my head, I might feel warm and fuzzy or run the risk of opening old wounds. But I'm really treading water. It's fun but unproductive and can be mentally exhausting.

Remember the movie *The Way We Were* with Robert Redford and Barbra Streisand? My favorite scene is on the sailboat when Redford and his college chum, Bradford Dillman, were naming all of the "best" memory moments in their lives. It's a feel-good moment of joy and gratitude for past memories. I've played the same game with a few close friends when we're drinking too much wine. It goes something like this: best Saturday afternoon, best month, best year. And you can make up any "best." Here are some of mine:

Best Month: November—my birthday and the month David asked me out

Best Year: 1961—I graduated from high school, entered college, found out I was Jewish, and dated my first Jew, the son of a cantor

Best Sunday: Sailing with Ben

Best One-Night Stand: Schlomo, the Israeli theater actor, who took me around Tel Aviv for the night and made love to me as if it was the last time we were going to have sex. I almost didn't make it to Egypt.

Best Big Sister: Carolyn

Best Business Partner: Maryan Stephens

Best Associate Artistic Director/Director: Philip McKinley

Best Movie: Too difficult to name one; but *Godfather I and II, The Maltase Falcon, Casablanca*. Really, really girly favorite: *Two for the Road*

Best Prom Dress: Senior ball and junior prom (it's a toss–up—my mother made them both). One was a copy from My Fair Lady, and the other was a copy of Maggie the Cat's dress (Elizabeth Taylor) in Cat on a Hot Tin Roof.

I recently saw the movie again and was struck by the end of the scene. After the litany of "bests," the two men look out at the ocean, and their connection to the past dissipates. They are lost to the pain of the present.

I was amazed that my friend Corrine never made a scrapbook during her thirty years of marriage. One day, I asked her if I could see pictures of her life together with her beloved husband who had died several years earlier.

"I don't have any pictures," she said with a characteristic twinkle in her eyes.

"Why not?" I gasped, thinking of the scrapbooks lining my closet floor and stuffed in drawers in my coffee table and the dozens of photos on my bookcase of my children and grandchildren.

"That's the past," she said casually. "I don't have pictures of the past around the house. But I have Dick in my heart now and forever. Anyway, he's always around the house."

She had one great picture of dashing Dick that was somewhat hidden behind a few random knickknacks, which may or may not have held much importance to her, the knickknacks, I mean.

Corinne got me thinking: Can we learn anything from our scrapbooks? How much joy do we get from bringing back memories of a simpler time, or as the song goes, "Has time rewritten every line ... can it be that we were all so simple then, could we, should we ..."? Memories can be confusing or painful; they can be seen through rose-colored glasses, or they can expose the cracks in the façade of time past. Maybe just for a moment, I want to wallow in the memory of my photos and get all choked up over how I was, the way we—my ex and I—were in the early years of marriage, or how my sons looked growing up.

Do I really need my scrapbooks to remind me of what does not exist any longer? I turn the page, and the memory is gone. The next page is yet another emotional distraction. I haven't yet mastered the art of detachment from my memories of David. There are still a few great memories that are keepers. I will always honor David's picture on my bookcase.

My mother started making photo albums and writing travel journals when my parents were just married and my father worked for the Southern Pacific Railroad in San Francisco. Throughout the 1930s and early 1940s, they were able to ride the train for free across the United States, including Mexico and Canada. I can't imagine what my brother and I will do with her scrapbooks when our mother dies. I love looking at my parents when they were young and glamorous, and I get emotional when I see them together—so much in love, so adventurous, so happy. My father, John, the long, strapping Irishman reminiscent of a young John Wayne, and my mother, Estelle, a dead-on look-alike for Carmen Miranda, with dark braids wrapped around her head, posing on thick corked high-heeled shoes, wearing a stylish tight suit. She is only missing the fruit on top of her head. The practical aspects of what to do with my mother's forty scrapbooks and remembrances are daunting.

INT. GARAGE - DAY

LANCE, JOAN's brother, opens the hope chest in the garage. Joan and Lance stare into the hope chest full to the top with scrapbooks.

                LANCE
They weigh a ton.

                JOAN
She even kept all the room keys ... no wonder they're heavy.

                LANCE
I almost broke my back lugging these out to the garage.

Joan opens several scrapbooks.

                JOAN
Maps ... menus ... theater stubs ...

Lance rummages through the books.

                LANCE
When did they invent color film? I only see black-and-white pictures.

                JOAN
These scrapbooks only go through 1952.

LANCE
Christ! Where are the rest? It's 2009.

JOAN
In the hope chest at the foot of her bed. The rest are under the cabinets in the TV room. Don't you look around the house?

LANCE
Not if I can help it.

JOAN
That's not nice.

LANCE
The contents of the house are yours, remember?

JOAN
What am I supposed to do with these?

LANCE
I suggest you leave them out on the sidewalk for the garbage to take them.

JOAN
I can't do that.

LANCE
Got any other ideas? What about your apartment?

> Joan is silent and seemingly resigned.
>
> LANCE
> No one said this was going to be easy.
>
> Joan and Lance stare at the hope chest, hopelessly.

I'm giving my scrapbooks to my adult children the next time I see them.

OH, BROTHER, WHERE ART THOU?

Although we are all born alone and die alone, living alone seems less ominous with the presence of my brother in my life. I've noticed that my connection with my brother is more important to me as I grow older. He knows my history, my predilections and idiosyncrasies, my children, even my thoughts. I trust him more than any person on earth. I don't know what I would do without his love and support, not to mention his help on financial matters. We've always conversed easily and acknowledged an unspoken subtext of all that that binds us together as a family.

Three years ago, my brother lost his wife of over forty years to cancer. And many decades ago, he lost his son Matthew at the young age of eighteen. It was a tragic accident and could have destroyed my brother and his wife, as well as Matthew's older brother, Philip. But Matthew's death did not destroy; his death solidified our faith and love in family and the dignity of life and death. My brother and his wife believed that Matthew's energy was released to the universe, and their collective love for him would provide strength in their lives. They were heroes and important role models in my life. When my brother's wife decided she did not want to prolong her life because chemo would not provide much hope, she accepted her death gracefully and passed into her final transition with ease, dignity, and divine grace. It was time for her to be with

Matthew. Because my brother's karma is amazing, he was recently given another angel. My new sister-in-law is as lovely a woman as one could find on earth.

LET'S HANG ON TO WHAT WE'VE GOT

I take up every space in my closet with my clothes. No one else lives in my apartment, and in point of fact, no one would be able to move in because there is no extra closet space. I've spread my clothes out so they are not packed inside like sardines.

Here is an axiom: if I buy an article of clothing, I must give away an article of clothing or at least take it to the resale store if it has a moderately good label on it. Most people are fiercely attached to old things and are reluctant to part with them. Women even hold on to their wedding dress so that they can pass it along to their daughter, who will surely want to get married in it someday. Do women actually think that's going to be a possibility in this day and age? A mother can't possibly compete with a wedding dress designed by Vera Wang.

I follow the giveaway clothes program religiously because I think it's creepy to keep clothes I wore decades ago. Do I want to keep the black turtleneck sweater when I was with what's his name in 1982? But the best reason for removing old clothes from my closet/s is that it is therapeutic. It feels cathartic, like getting a high colonic or gorging on Godiva chocolate.

Here is my quick lesson in clothes therapy: I go through my closet and try on everything I think I might want to get rid of. I don't keep clothes that I cannot fit in any longer. It's a waste of time to keep them because at sixty-four, the likelihood that I'll fit in those size 2 jeans again is 1,000 to 1. Size doesn't matter; it's better to feel comfortable in clothes. Thinking that I should wear a particular size is judgmental and counterproductive to a healthy mind-set. It is time to get a grip on body image! I don't model for *Vogue*.

I go through my closet a second time and pull out the clothes that are out of style. Those are usually the same clothes that don't fit anymore: too-tight sweaters, too-tight skirts, and anything that resembles short shorts. Too-tight anything means I'll be self-conscious and won't enjoy dinner with a date. I look at the belly shirts with longing for the time I actually could wear them without embarrassment. I wouldn't think of showing my stomach unless it was flat, and that is a distant memory. In fact, showing any skin around the midsection for anyone over sixty is one step away from suicide. I try to wear flattering colors, usually black and white, and I stay away from trendy youth-oriented apparel.

Once a year, usually around autumn, I created a fashion show for David and modeled the clothes for him that I was almost sure looked ghastly on me. As my mother used to say, I was weeding out the bad to make room for what looks good on my ever-changing body. David would sit on the couch watching Sunday football as I modeled coats, jackets, shoes, dresses, skirts, and hats I never wore anymore.

INT. JOAN'S APARTMENT - LATE AFTERNOON
JOAN enters the living room in a 1990s dress. DAVID sits on the couch, watching television.

                    DAVID
        (with a deadpan expression)
    Lose it.

                    JOAN
    Lose it?

                    DAVID
    You asked me ...

                    JOAN
    But don't you think the ruffles on
    the skirt are kinda flouncy and
    fun?

> DAVID
>
> Lose it.
>
> JOAN
>
> It still works ...
>
> DAVID
>
> You asked me what I thought.
>
> JOAN
>
> Right. I asked you.
>
> DAVID
> (looks back at the TV)
>
> I just missed the play.
>
> JOAN
>
> You'll see it on instant replay.
>
> DAVID
>
> It's not the same.
>
> David's eyes slowly drift back to Joan.
>
> DAVID
>
> Next.
>
> Joan walks back into her bedroom, head down, not happy.

I adored that David participated in this silly ritual with me. He was my personal clothes trainer. We both liked to live light and kept very little in terms of personal inventory. We had the philosophy that clutter created chaos and obscured the peaceful feeling of space and light in our environment. An uncluttered environment is not appealing to everyone, and I thoroughly understand the need to hold on and attach to favorite things. Nevertheless, I never miss an article of clothing or shoes when I donate them to the abused women's shelter or give them to the women at the recovery center where I teach yoga and meditation. I know that everything I give to another woman is going to be worn with joy and gratitude. My mantra is "Everything is borrowed or rented in life." So since we don't actually own anything, I can give my things to someone else in need. I've already given away the contents of a house.

The "pay it forward" philosophy keeps gratitude and compassion alive. A year before my mother died, I was visiting her in Las Vegas, and she miraculously remembered that, decades ago, I had given her a magnificent abstract wood carving. "It's called *The Pregnant Woman*," she casually said. Minutes before, she could not remember that my brother's first wife had died of cancer two and a half years ago. I was momentarily stunned.

"Yes, and I remember that my ex was furious that I gave the sculpture to you," I added.

"Oh, I remember that too," she said with a twinkle in her eye.

I looked around her home and realized that I had given my mother many pieces of art, and they fit comfortably in her home. I didn't want them back.

Things are entirely what they appear to be
And behind them ... there is nothing.
—Sartre

CURIOSITY DID NOT KILL THE CAT

One of the blessings of living alone is that I have more time and opportunity to become more curious about expanding my views on life and living. I think that over time, people become myopic about their living experience. It's often challenging to go outside the prescribed boundaries of their lives and explore other options. Resistance is the killer of curiosity. When I am curious, I am challenged to go outside my comfort zone by engaging in activities that I might not have thought of in the past. To be curious takes effort and practice, and let's face it, most of us have lazy minds. However, my ability to be more curious brings more meaning and pleasure to each day; it affects my moods, my thoughts, and my actions.

I am curious about travel, about books, about people, about events. I am curious to explore new ideas and philosophies and even new dances. I can't wait to take a hip-hop class. I cannot tell you the number of friends and clients who have expressed the desire to learn salsa or swing, try hip-hop, study a musical instrument, take up photography, or give time to charitable activities. These activities spread joy and create positive energy. I have another saying on my refrigerator door.

Eliminate something superfluous from your life.
Break a habit.
Do something that makes you feel insecure.
Carry out an action with complete attention and intensity,
As if it were your last.

—*Piero Ferrucci,*
psychotherapist and philosopher

Part of being curious is to do something different that I have not done before. It's exciting to challenge myself. When I actually cook a meal for myself, I am moving outside my comfort zone, doing something I am not expected to do. It means that I take time to call a friend who does not expect hearing from me, even when I'm not feeling up to it because I am rushing all day from class to class. I may suddenly stop everything because I feel the need to meditate and clear my mind of clutter. When I do something unexpected and fulfilling, I give myself a gift.

I have always believed that a truly effective antiaging technique, as well as a mood elevator, is to speed up thinking during the day. The aging process often slows down the mind. I am aware that I am not as sharp as I once was. Struggling for words can be downright embarrassing. Counteracting a sluggish mind increases energy and creativity. Everyone knows by now the old adage about keeping the mind sharp by doing crossword puzzles. I must confess I'm terrible at them, but I remember vividly my ex-mother-in-law doing puzzles into her eighties. Her mind was still active and sharp before she died. She was always a curious woman.

My mother, unfortunately, did not keep her mind active and did not stay curious and I saw the results in later on in her life. Brain inactivity exacerbates dementia and short-term memory loss. It was painful to see my mother lose her ability to think. She never placed a premium on intellectual curiosity, nor had she been one to go deeper into the psychology of the mind. Therefore, it is my intention to keep my brain active and functioning through mindful awareness.

I just read an article in the *Los Angeles Times* a list of things that can prevent the mind from slowing down. At the top of the list was stretching and exercise. I jumped for joy! I don't have to do crossword puzzles, although that is the second item on the anti-aging list. I'm actively engaged in the number one, top-of-the-list activity for preventing the onset of dementia. Stretching, walking, dancing—any form of physical activity strengthens the mind. The added benefit of physical activity, especially stretching and walking, is a more positive attitude toward life. It is truly amazing that something so simple to do, costing virtually nothing, brings more joy and less stress to living and, at the same time, adds to the overall mental and physical health of people.

FORGET YOUR TROUBLES, COME ON, GET HAPPY

Despite my protestations and whining during this aging process, I place great value on an optimistic and positive approach to life. I am usually in a good mood, so it is really difficult for me to tolerate a person who gives off negative energy, but I try to counter the downer mood with my own positive energy. When I suspect an unhappy person approaching me—usually with a scowl on the face, pinched eyes, and a guarded demeanor—I approach with caution. These downer people are difficult to embrace on a daily basis. They are usually all about themselves. Spreading negativity and collecting injustices are part of their program, but I try to muster up all the positive energy I have in my body and make the encounter tolerable. When it's over, I move on with appropriate speed.

Studies have shown that our good moods increase our ability to bring happiness to others by doing good deeds. Performing a small act of kindness once or twice a day lifts our spirits. I am always conscious about thanking the checker or the bagger at the grocery store and giving them a smile and a "Have a good day" before leaving. I remind myself to say "Excuse me" as I pass too close to someone in the aisles or accidently bump someone in the airport. I take a friend out to dinner for no reason at all. I call a friend or acquaintance to say I am thinking about him/her, I call or visit someone who is sick, and I express compassion when a friend tells me about a personal problem.

It is important for my soul and my physical, mental, and emotional being to devote some time during my day to doings things that give me pleasure. Of course, it's almost impossible for me to do that since teaching yoga is the most pleasurable experience in my day, and my teaching releases endorphins that keep me on a perpetual high. However, I do need some personal pleasure other than yoga to counterbalance the routine activities of my job or domestic responsibilities in the home. The pleasure I give myself is like changing the sheets on my bed. When I lie down between the sheets on my bed, they engulf me with freshness.

This is yet another list. Things that make me happy are the following:

Taking a daily walk alone or with a friend

Finding a buddy to partner with at the gym if we don't like to go alone

Getting a facial or a mani/pedi

Taking an extra five minutes to meditate, to breathe deeply

Making a resolution to eat better and to drink more water (dehydration makes a person lethargic)

Eating the good fats: avocado, olive oil, and nuts

Taking flaxseed oil for the eyes and skin

Planning a short trip on the weekend to a winery, the beach, the mountains, or a mall

Selecting a different restaurant to dine and sampling a new atmosphere and food

Meeting up with friends

"Friend power" is another way of achieving happiness. Social relationships, a gathering with a group of our important friends, releases endorphins, excites the nervous system in a positive way, challenges our minds, and opens our hearts. I realize there are introverts who are not inclined to socialize with people, and it may be a little difficult to get out of the apartment or house, but it can be positive and uplifting emotionally and psychologically to be close to other people. I am an extrovert, and I have other challenges like putting my foot in my mouth from time to time. Extroverts may tell people too often what we really think. We even talk to strangers! Our happiness and joy comes from many places in our universe. Sometimes we are all over the map of life.

One of the most important aspects to living a positive life is to set up a happy environment. Favorite colors, beautiful furniture pieces, plants, music, and smells all contribute to our aesthetic pleasure and create a background that brings us closer to our emotional needs. I wanted to paint one of my walls in my apartment a fabulous marigold color as an accent to my institutional white apartment walls. I asked my theater friend if he would do it for me because I knew it would be a disaster if I painted anything. Of course, he came over and did the job like a professional. He also got a home-cooked meal. The new color and my friend brightened my spirits.

A special word about music: music is one of the most important and special treats in my life. I love jazz, tango music, world music, Buddhist chants, Steely Dan, and Spanish guitars. Music has never failed to lift my spirits. When living alone brings me too much solitude, I put on my favorite music. It's my best friend.

Just recently, I thought about setting up a new environment in my brain. I was disturbed by my propensity to continually replay the old tapes, the old negative thoughts in my head. These inner monologues were obviously not going to enhance my positive mood. Too much stress and anxiety were building up. I never realized how many times a day I utter negative thoughts about myself, as well as other people, places, and/or things. It was becoming an unconscious habit. Staying present, staying mindful is vital to keep my state of being positive. So I made one of my ever-expanding lists:

I noted all the negative thoughts I had during the day.

I asked myself, where do these thoughts come from?

I asked, how do these thoughts make me feel?

I restated the negative statements.

I made them positive.

My negative thought is as follows: *I'm such a loser when it comes to men.*

I am not really a loser. Okay, I had a few men who wouldn't/couldn't commit, whose mother complex prevented them from leaving their real or psychic mother and embracing the love of a woman. Maybe I wasn't the right woman. Maybe they lacked sufficient passion for me.

Rephrase: I've met some men who were not right for me. It was hurtful at first; then, I realized that it was negative to want a man who wasn't ready for me or who was not individuated enough to form a bond with a woman he loves or thinks he loves.

THE BEST REVENGE

Sixteenth-century English clergyman and metaphysical poet George Herbert said:

Living well is the best revenge.

Herbert's quote does not refer to punishing others or going after retribution for personal harm. Nor does it refer to coloring your hair. I'm sure the clergyman was speaking about the values people choose to live by throughout their lives; in short, he was probably referring to living life with an open heart and following a code of ethical and spiritual behavior that fosters forgiveness.

It is not an easy task to live well. I can see it in the faces of people I pass every day. Very few people are smiling. It is off-putting to see unhappy people pursing their lips together and wearing faces so tense it appears there is blockage somewhere in their derriere. People who sport frown lines or scowls are just plain annoying. Maybe these people need a little Botox to release their inner monologue.

Wearing a great smile sends positive energy into the universe, and smiling has a definite effect on our endorphins. A smile connotes a happy interior life and a willingness to spread joy to others. If I walk down the grocery aisle smiling, the person I pass returns my smile. I also smile when I practice my daily meditation. It really does add to the happiness quotient. Some Buddhists monks do it that way, and I have never seen an unhappy, unsmiling Buddhist.

The chaos and pessimistic images shaping the world intrudes daily on my thoughts and actions and sometimes gets in the way of my living well. My therapist, Mike, suggests that I eliminate the trendy obsessive thinking of the collective unconscious and decide what the right and appropriate course of action might be for me. This is a difficult task since I am inundated with other people's opinions, which are filtered through social, cultural, and political agendas. I think it's fair to say that when I don't think for myself and become mentally lazy, I am often overwhelmed by irrational fears. I begin to feel that people are all merely extensions of each other.

I know I'm not like everyone else, but I don't want to find myself in the middle of a herd of sheep that collectively thinks as one. It's dangerous and it perpetuates fear and self-loathing. That's when the lemmings all walk off the cliff together. The most effective way to reduce any negative impact is to stay focused on my own life and not try to move institutional mountains.

HERE COMES DA JUDGE

Since there isn't much conversation outside of my work, I rely too frequently on my inner monologue for validation of my opinions and thoughts. Mike, the yogis, and the people in the know about inner work have suggested practicing nonjudging. Judging is a reversion to an immature state, to the little girl or little boy inside of us. If I free myself from judgment, I am capable of responding with greater clarity and wisdom, and I can love myself more than I thought possible. Honoring the divine within myself (namaste) releases me from the collective unconscious, which in turn eliminates the impulses and irrational fears of my youth and even adulthood. In essence, my cathartic release activates the pleasure centers of my brain and affects my mind, the entity I know as myself.

Beware of the judgers in life. They are everywhere. They are our children, our friends, our relatives, our coworkers, our spouses, and our parents. They pose no threat. They are not our minds, our feelings, or our actions. Let's just get out of the way of those who judge and behold our path.

SHEDDING MY SKIN: SNAKES DO IT

I was driving to my dentist and had a thought about being alone: It hurts so good to be alone. I have the freedom to make my own decision. I have the freedom to go to the movies on Saturday afternoon without asking anyone, to walk the hills on Sunday with Annie, or to go to the Wooden Center and work on my favorite cardio machine. I have the freedom to take a yin yoga class on Sundays. I have the freedom to spend time with one of my best guy friends and get some male energy around me. I have the freedom to eat what I want from Whole Foods or to get a burrito from Baja Fresh. I have the freedom to spend the entire Sunday morning at Abbot's Habit in Venice and sit in the company of hippies and beatniks over breakfast and read the paper or write my book. I have the freedom to go to Las Vegas to visit my family any weekend I choose, to sit with my mother in silence as she stares at the television, or to take my grandsons to swim class, basketball, or soccer practice.

Being alone gives me the gift of time to work on growth and change. I have the opportunity to meditate, empty my mind, release my fears and realize that inner peace is the only path that allows me to open my heart to myself and to others. I am able to find clarity in my relationship with my psyche, my soul, as well as release the vestiges of those old parental messages and resist cultural messages that inhibit my personal growth. I am free to contemplate self-mastery as a way to gain enlightenment.

I start each day with gratitude for all the gifts in my life: my family, my work as a yoga teacher, my beloved friends, and all the people I meet along the way in tango, in yoga circles, every checker at Whole Foods, every barista at Starbucks, and all those whom I will meet in the future.

Every night, I have a ritual: I go out on my balcony and offer gratitude and embrace the awesomeness of the universe. I have learned that the more gratitude I give in life, the more gifts will be returned. The beauty of gratitude encompasses forgiveness, and forgiveness encompasses joy, and joy breeds more joy and enriches life to its fullest.

That's what my yoga master meant when he said, "Follow your bliss."

Text message from my supervisor at UCLA, Elisa
can u sub M/W noon
1 hr class nice group
may need perm sub
I'll get ur classes covered
cm on cell thx, E
ps Columbus didn't discover America
no holiday 2day

CHAPTER 12
GOTTA GET OUT OF DODGE

I am very fortunate to have my job. I can't believe that I am a yoga instructor in my sixties. I am in a state of amazement and wonder. I'm honoring my body, mind, and spirit as a teacher and as a practitioner and meditating daily. I have less stress, more serenity. I also added drug counselor to this mix because I believe that yoga and meditation enhance the spiritual connection to the recovery journey.

I never actually planned a career trajectory with any sense of rational thinking. For half of my life, it was the theater that captured my heart and soul. During the rest of my so-called career, I haphazardly fell into several professions by accident—some great, some not so great. If there was a centerpiece to my working journey, it was teaching. My mother used to say to me, "Joanie, you're a born teacher. You ought to stick with it. Besides, you're very funny."

THE GREATEST SHOW ON EARTH

Once upon a time, when I was eight years old, my parents took me to the movies to see *The Greatest Show on Earth* with Cornel Wilde, Betty Hutton, and Charlton Heston. It was a story about people in the circus. I fell in love with the movies and dreamed of being a trapeze artist for years after, but I thought that would be an over-the-top idea for my mother to swallow. With my visible chipped tooth and fuzzy curly hair, I switched careers as we walked out of the Rafael movie theater.

"I want to be a movie star," I said to my mother with finite conviction.

"You can be anything you want, honey," she said to me.

Wow! Did my mother say that to me in 1952? She was a feminist ahead of her time and a woman of independent thought and conviction.

I didn't become the movie star I had envisioned, and it really didn't matter in the long run. The universe and my parents gave me the uncanny ability to land on my feet when the going got tough. Those years of teaching high school drama and theater classes in college, acting, and running my own year-round professional theater were productive from a career standpoint; and I was happy. When I left Las Vegas, theater became a means to make a living rather than my passion.

Theater was a profession chosen out of love and strong emotion until my crazy zest for living outside the artifice of the theater world lead me away from the eight-year-old little girl who wanted to be an actress. But the soul of an artist never dies, and film school gave me back my artistic passion. Writing became my muse. In the years of raising children and holding down the domestic front with David, writing kept me sane and provided focus.

And then another mystery befell me. Even though times were lean with financial issues holding front and center, I migrated to a yoga studio and found salvation. I took a yoga teacher–training course without much thought as to what I was going to do with it except deepen my practice. Then one day, I quit or got fired or both from the brokerage firm and started teaching yoga, and I was the happiest I have ever been in my life. One yoga studio job led to another. I got a few private clients, signed up at UCLA athletic department, got a drug counseling license; and my so-called career finally gelled after twenty-five years. Sometimes the Irish luck kicked along with good karma. David used to say that luck was the intersection of timing and opportunity.

TIMBUKTU AND OTHER PLACES TO HIDE

From time to time, my need for variety and excitement produced a kind of wanderlust. I call it a virus because it gets inside of me, holding on so tight that it causes me to fantasize about living in other places on the planet and celebrating life by doing hugely significant work for others. I blame my wanderlust on my job as an ESL teacher. Teaching English as a second language to people around the world gave my imagination a workout.

I dreamed of traveling to Timbuktu to work in a children's orphanage or teach English to schoolchildren or help out the small medical team that visited once a month.

I fantasized that I could teach English as a second language in Buenos Aires and dance tango every night. I imagined I would drag my tired body into executive offices after dancing all night and teach English to handsome Argentine men in dark pin-striped suits and wide silk ties. It would be difficult to concentrate on the task at hand for obvious reasons; that is, exhaustion from dancing tango most of the night. I would no doubt run out of gas in three months.

At one point, I explored the possibility of becoming a global volunteer with an eye on finding an ESL position. I thought long and hard about taking a job at a Buddhist monastery in a remote part of Thailand where I would teach English to monks in orange robes, whose joy it was to daily intone chants to the great Buddha. I saw myself as the only woman sitting in a very large room chanting "om" for hours at a time and then convening into a smaller room lit by natural light, where I would teach English syntax for two hours a day to monks who had no idea why it was necessary for them to learn the English language. They never talked to each other anyway, and if they did, it was in Thai or Sanskrit.

I had the brilliant idea that I could take my closet full of film scripts and my two published textbooks on acting to a California women's prison and teach drama to the inmates. Previously, I used some of the themes in my film scripts as ideas for improvisation/role-playing in my AIDS education groups at a California women's prison. I imagined that I might also be able to teach lesbians Argentine tango as it relates to one of my screenplays. The idea of filling a prison room and adjacent cells with tango music was thrilling.

TIME IN A BOTTLE

I just turned sixty-five. Medicare card in hand, a signatory to an HMO, and I've just lost half my retirement funds. There is no defense against greed and stupidity. It's the human condition, and it never loses its appeal. When the herd mentality sets in, and fear raises its ugly head, we all hear the shrieks of "poor me" from the Wall Street warriors. Vile corruption deserves no mercy. I won't follow the lemmings and sell the rest of my nest egg. What goes down will come up. Yada, yada, yada.

In the beginning, I felt oddly detached watching the stock market plummet. It felt like a movie was running through my head. I was watching it, but not connecting to the narrative in any conscious sense. For a time, I thought this was going to be someone else's problem. Then it hit me like a sledgehammer. Like Rip Van Winkle, I awakened after twenty years of sleep to find a world that had changed—and not for the better. And I realized that I was going to work until I was seventy-five if my body could hold out. It's all about the practice of the Tao, daily losing.

For a time, my mind remained calm, but I am a flawed human being. I lost my yogic center as my stomach rumbled and then erupted like a volcano as I realized almost half my savings was gone. Worse, the "shoulda, woulda, coulda" thinking enveloped my being. Hindsight is an exact science. Nobody likes a Monday morning quarterback even if it is my brother doing the quarterbacking. I should have, when given the opportunity nine months earlier, converted everything in to Triple A tax-free treasury bonds like my brother told me to; but 8 percent seemed much better than 3.5 percent for the next couple of years. I could have sold off and still been in good shape—that is, if I had been paying attention to the market and not working all the time so I wouldn't need to dip into my retirement money prematurely. See how this backward thinking works? Time referencing is a negative preoccupation.

I needed to change my perspective in order to counterbalance the vagaries of my unbalanced mind. I was beginning to imagine myself pushing a cart around the Third Street Promenade in Santa Monica as early as next year. I wondered if I had enough warm clothing to ward off those infrequent below-fifty-degree nights along the beach.

"Don't worry, Mom," my son Jonathan said to me on the phone as I spoke to him outside the NanosSystems Institute on UCLA campus.

I was hyperventilating before going into the building to teach a yoga class to an outstanding group who expected better of me. I'm a yogini for God's sake! It's not good for a yoga teacher to have shortness of breath and negative energy surging through her body. Stress and anxiety are definitely not compatible with deep yoga breathing, with *prana*—the life force that allows us to keep our practice mindful, our bodies light, and our mind tranquil.

> *Bring the breath deep down into the belly, expand the rib cage on the inhale, contract the rib cage on the exhale, expel all the breath out. Note the gaps between the breath for moments of pure meditation.*

Breathing brought me back to consciousness. I had to snap out of it. I was listening to my son on my cell phone.

"Why don't you worry about something important? You know you've got two sons who will take care of you. I gotta get back to work. Talk to you over the weekend. Love you."

Jonathan hung up. I was totally and completely unsatisfied in that moment. No, darling sons, I worked so you wouldn't have to take care of me. You, dear children, don't understand what my main motivation has been in the last twenty years. No handouts, no dole.

I called Aaron, hoping for a different result, but what was it that I wanted from my sons? Aaron was Mr. Cool and equally unimpressed by my financial loss as his brother.

"Remember what David said," Aaron quipped back to me.

"No, what did David say, Aaron? Do tell," I lethargically asked.

"It's only money. They're still printing it."

I finally saw some humor. I snapped out of it, thinking about what David would have said on the subject of greed at this moment! He had no fear about life or its machinations.

"Fear is useless, irrational, created by people who project onto others their own worst fears so they will always be in the right, so they won't be found out for the frauds that they are," he would muse. "And payback is a bitch."

I walked into the NanoSystems building with a vague understanding of how I arrived in the middle of my sixties with a feeling of confusion and discontent. We have no script, no playbook to follow when things don't go well. Life's journey isn't linear; it's complicated, sad, confusing, joyful, and, once in a while, hopeful.

Note to myself: I have to be a better student of my messy life, understand my struggle, and provide my own consolation. Follow it up with acceptance. I'm not going to graduate from life with honors, but if I stay connected to being conscious, I can handle life's stumbling blocks.

I thought about Eckhart Tolle's books as my guides to gaining self-mastery and controlling the energy of my ego. I reread my yellow highlights in both books. I remembered what I had forgotten.

DON'T PUT YOUR LABEL ON ME

The economic state of our country and of the world at large threw me a curveball. I had forgotten to implement a few valuable techniques that had helped me stay present and balanced in the past. Staying conscious begins and ends with nonattachment, nonjudgment, and nonresistance. Somewhere in this mix is the huge option that "this too will pass." I did not do a very good job of avoiding the urge to trap myself inside events and situations on the economic front until I managed to find balance again by staying above the fray with a new mantra.

The three *nons*:

Nonattachment: I had to remember that I was a news junkie—reading, listening, and watching everything I could about the economic crisis. MSNBC, CNBC, CNN. My thoughts were boxed inside my head with no relief, and I couldn't let go. I had to step away and resist drowning in the craziness of the moment. I meditated with a vengeance in order to empty my mind, to resist negative thinking, and to detach from the incessant throbbing in my brain.

Nonjudgment: I judged every fluctuation of the Dow as positive or negative as it related to myself. I knew the economic situation had derailed my financial plans, and I wasn't getting back to near normal for a long time. And everyone on Wall Street and in Washington was carrying around labels, and the political scene seemed as polarized as ever. "I'm a Democratic; I'm a Republican. My side is always right." This labeling game created a judging free-for-all that never let up. I had to extricate myself from the judging and blaming because it was taking over my life.

Nonresistance: Politics is tied to economics, and both were putting me into a mental hammerlock. I needed to surrender because there was no getting out of Dodge. Dodge was everywhere. Sitting inside the situation and dis-identifying with the economic downturn was my only line of defense. Those other people—the greedy, stupid people—in charge of making bad decisions for the country were not me. There was another collective unconscious wrapping around the universe that provided compatibility and solace.

THE DREADED "R" WORD

The morning I woke up and finally acknowledged that I was in fact sixty-five, I had given the idea of retirement more or less some vague consideration. My vamp on this topic was, "I'll think about it tomorrow at Tara." *Gone with the Wind's* Scarlett O'Hara, the tenacious daughter of an Irish potato farmer, reflected my sentiments. My identity is half wrapped up in Scarlett's psyche. The Jewish half is the planner and executor of goals, and I'm the Dolly Levi in *Hello, Dolly!* who manifests success. Both ethnicities are dreamers, and both are diligent workers. Both film characters encompass the artistic and the pragmatic, and both personas are deeply imbedded in who I am and what I am becoming.

I'm so compelled by this idea of finding a sense of worth through work and creative outlets that I find it difficult to understand a woman who does not put her skill set to use in some capacity. My dearest yogi friend, Kathy, technically does not work. But Kathy is a wife, mother of adult children, a grandmother and part-time caretaker to her autistic grandson, a pillar of St. Matthew's Episcopal Church and School, it's head fund-raiser, a dedicated yogi, a daughter who has full responsibility of her ninety-five-year-old mother, and is involved in the care of her elderly in-laws. That's more than I can chew off in a decade. She also visits the sick and comforts those in her parish who have suffered loss because of death. I am sure Kathy does not consider any of this work, but she energizes to full capacity, and she is sixty-eight years old. She is my role model and my hero. The word "retirement" is not in her vocabulary and not on her lips. "Retire from what? Life?" she purrs with her angelic voice.

Work is a state of amazement and wonder. I am renewed each day by its accessibility to the divine and its connectedness to human nature. It keeps me conscious and balanced. It is true that not everyone enjoys the work he or she does in life. There were times I thought I could not endure one more minute in a brokerage office trying to look busy or attempting to create a new marketing idea.

Before my encounter with yoga and the concept of mindfulness and balance, I would go a little crazy with the old tape: "Why me?" "Why am I here?" "How did I end up making the choice to be here?" "I don't deserve this kind of treatment," "How can I get out of this job with dignity and earn money to live?" "Where did I go wrong?" "How am I going to survive?" This kind of doomsday thinking is, to say the least, negative and directly opposed to the positive life force within me. It took me six months before I could remember that there is always light inside the darkness. That's when I took up teaching yoga.

More than a few days in the last year, I heard myself say, "when I retire." I was actually saying this over and over again, especially through months of burnout at work. I was encountering scheduling problems with classes, cancellations with clients, and my aging mother's condition. I worried about my stressed-out brother. I seemed to be slowly crumbling with excuses so I could get out of Dodge.

What a very nasty word the "R" word can be. If the "R" word was going to define the boundaries of my life in my midsixties, I was going to go down a negative road that could limit and shackle my journey. I henceforth banned the "R" word.

Boomers, for the most part, are not going to retire. At least, they are not going to retire to a rocking chair full-time. Boomers are inclined to move on to the next part of their lives if their jobs come to an end. As we know, these days jobs can come to an end prematurely faster than you can say "Ready, set, retire."

Some boomers will take their social security early, usually at sixty-two or sixty-three (most can take social security at sixty-six or sixty-seven) when there are few job openings for people over sixty. After all, what corporation wants to take on the aches and pains of what they perceive to be an over-the-hill sixty-two-year-old worker? For those who are in self-employed positions like financial planners, owners of businesses, real estate agents, or professionals who provide services in law, medicine, health, or education, there will be flexibility in deciding when to retire or partially retire. However, there will be some boomers who choose to take care of aging parents and must leave their jobs because they cannot afford the high costs of convalescent centers. Others are so burned out, like my neighbor who taught in the Los Angeles Unified School District for thirty-eight years that she decided to retire at sixty-one or end up in a lunatic asylum.

Unfortunately, more boomers are going to feel the pinch of financial insecurity as they see their 401(k)s hit unprecedented lows, and they figure out very quickly that retirement is going to be deferred. Those who had to cash in stocks that have hit historic lows in order to afford college tuition or pay off balloon payments on assets or have lived too high on the hog for decades and have to sell their toys, deferred retirement is a probability.

The fact is that at sixty-five, my daily yoga teaching takes a toll on my body and leads me into premature exhaustion before the week is over. I try not to think about how my muscles will be sore before Friday, but I take each day as a blessing and a gift. I know I have even more energy within myself to continue. Before the financial crash reared its ugly head, I began to figure out that I would have to work longer because it was a good plan to keep earning. I was going to work several years past sixty-six, even with social security available to me. So, the financial crisis just validated on my plan. I'm now visualizing working until seventy.

WITH RETIREMENT, YOU GET EGG ROLL

What does life after sixty-five look like? Approximately 78 million American baby boomers—the first of whom will turn sixty-five next year—are now beginning to retire. More than half are interested in starting new careers. The real surprise is that boomers are exploring job options that have social impact. This new trend may turn out to be the ubiquitous boomer anti-aging serum. To a generation that was once on the cutting edge of changing the world, it seems passé to put all that energy on improving that golf game. There are countless examples of doctors, scientists, engineers, lawyers, and businessmen carving out new paths for themselves and giving back to their communities in the form of green innovation, education, and community-based programming. This encore career work matters not just for the boomers, but also for the health and welfare of our country. Besides, it's probably a heck of a lot more fun than their first career track because it's a give-back-feel-good path that reflects attitudes and emotions of the 1960s revolution.

There is a new trend today that is of interest to boomers who are either retiring by choice or by force. For a man or woman who has devoted thirty years or more to a job, future dreams require time and money. A friend told me that he wants to work a three-quarter week and have some freedom to pursue his passion for travel. Another has always had a dream of training for a triathlon. But some of us either cannot negotiate a reduced work schedule or cannot find another business to develop that provides sufficient income and gives us the personal time we need to fulfill our passions. Perhaps, it seems that the definition of "retirement" in its old-fashioned connotation is almost obsolete in these times.

I recently read about a phenomenon among boomers who own mobile homes. Some of these folks are early retirees, some have been let go from jobs, and some have reached maximum retirement. Some are single men and women, and some are couples, married or not. Their one common interest is saving national parks and recreation areas around the country. They travel to a particular park—for example, to Texas or Colorado or the Dakotas—and stay for four or five months at a time and work as volunteer replacements for the thousands of park employees who had to be let go. The one unifying common goal of these RV seniors is to keep the national parks open and provide services to visitors. They lead trail walks and bird-watching expeditions, keep the park facilities clean, gather garbage, and do whatever it takes to keep the fabric of our national park system functioning. Mobile home rent is very reasonable, and small perks are given to them for their volunteer work. But the most important perks are the long-standing friendships that are made along the way, from park to park, from state to state. Information is exchanged among the senior volunteers about the status of a variety of park facilities, and folks always make plans to meet again several times a year to cement their bonds.

Another way of handling retirement is to solicit the help of a retirement coach. This coaching industry was developed out of a need for boomers, people in their late fifties and sixties, to address the endemic layoff and burnouts persistently present in our society. There are also men and women who are choosing not to work full-time and want to explore part-time opportunities in the business world. Coaches use a variety of personality assessment tools, ask the client a long list of questions, and help boomers focus on what they really want to do in the next phase of their lives, even if the idea seems out of the normal range of traditional work. Although the coach can spend an exhausting few months collecting data and gathering personal information for the client, in the end, the coach cannot provide the client with definitive answers. The client has to do the hard work of making the final decision. Finding productive work on the back nine is a process of discovery. Boomers will potentially live well into their eighties; and that twenty-year stretch of time can increase the quality of life not only physically, but, more importantly, mentally. To find a retirement coach, go to http://www.coachfederation.org.

What happens to people who are fortunate enough to retire today without having to return to work or perhaps have the luxury of working part-time? People who choose to work in a limited capacity also have time on their hands. I'm thinking of my daughter-in-law's parents. Saul still works as a lawyer, but for a while, he considered leaving his business until he realized he needed to continue to practice law in order to survive psychologically and emotionally and to extend his earning years. Yet, at sixty-one, he is more than willing to join his wife's incredible adventure in living. He and Marlene are making their lives full and fun by traveling around the world and satisfying their sense of curiosity and continued education about other cultures. I have friends who take a cruise each year to learn about other countries and explore places they have always wanted to visit.

But suppose people do not have sufficient disposable income to create their retirement in this manner. How can they retire happy, wild, and free?

There is a book out that I recommend to retirees who want to relocate. Barbara Corcoran wrote a book called *Nextville, Amazing Places to Live the Rest of Your Life.* Corcoran, with her cowriter, Warren Berger, offers practical information and insights based on national surveys and numerous interviews referencing real people and places for the next boomer movement. *Nextville* features one hundred national and international destinations and includes ballpark estimates of real estate costs, climates, and population. This book actually helps boomers think outside the box when it comes to organizing a new direction for life in the sixties.

Warning: This book is not for the faint of heart or for those who have issues with change. A sense of true adventure is required. Corcoran's book is a cogent analysis that matches the reader's interests to any direction they favor in regard to movement or relocation.

I'm definitely excited about entertaining different places to live, and Nextville gave me plenty of food for thought. I don't want to live in a crowded urban setting in a high-rise condo. I definitely do not want to huddle with a group of people for any length of time because gathering friends and like-minded people together to form a twenty-first-century version of a commune is too-1968 retro. My cannabis-loving ex-brother-in-law did that in Laurel Canyon and has long since traveled a highly individualist road decades before he was sixty-five. I actually got excited about a lifestyle that divides my time between two preferred places. Who knows what the future holds for my family, but I could conceivably walk that line between two cities to visit family. I might even enjoy the experience of trading locations every couple of months.

Retirement is not just about getting advice from your financial consultant, says Ernie J. Zelinski in his informative book *How to Retire Happy, Wild, and Free*. Mr. Zelinski constructs creative retirement scenarios about living large in the last decades of life that are as clear and interesting.

Mr. Zelinski concludes that there is no such thing as retirement. A person does not retire from the human race when one leaves a job. A person just begins to live happy, wild, and free at retirement age. Go to the Web site joyofnotworking.com if you don't believe me, and you will never be bored or depressed. I got to page 71 in Zelinski's book and stared at the subtitle: Not Writing a Book Can Be More Difficult than Writing One. He was telling the truth. I'm a writer and have written all my life—whether it be program notes in my theater playbills, speeches, articles, plays, screenplays, textbooks, or a novel. They may not have been all great, but it was the best effort I had in me at the time. Writing is a therapeutic process, a creative endeavor that can electrify the soul and stir passions. It's an adrenaline rush, a dopamine flush, and a serotonin infusion that you will get nowhere else except maybe in a yoga practice.

The mantra of Zelinski's book and other retirement books on the market is that in retirement, people have the opportunity to achieve more meaning and purpose in their lives than they ever thought possible. Reclaiming the individual creative spirit later in life may just be the best part of life. My neighbor Diane discovered she is a professional-level photographer. Who knew, but retirement gave her the opportunity to find out.

I just read an article in the *Los Angeles Times* on Sunday that described a senior community in Southern California. The array of activities to do inside the community is absolutely astounding. Sure, there is bingo; but now there is bocce ball, ping-pong, shuffleboard, billiards, a library, card games, pinochle, hiking, music, swimming, art appreciation, movies, a parapsychology club, and the Life after Life Club. One woman said, "It's God's waiting place." Single people and couples are welcome, and all walks of life blend effortlessly in these community living centers.

The new trend in senior living is niche communities. Because the baby boomer population control 70 percent of the wealth in the United States, the proliferation of retirement housing market will cause massive changes in the future. Niche community living based on group interest is becoming a popular trend. For now, niche housing represents a small portion of senior housing today, probably less than 1 percent. However, thirty years from now, niche housing will be the norm.

An important factor in this future growth paradigm is the psychological and emotional need to be near others with like backgrounds and interests.

The following is a representative sampling of niche senior communities:

For artists and poets: Burbank Senior Artists Colony provides an art studio, theater complex, writing and poetry classes, choir, and a Hollywood-themed clubhouse for chat sessions. The National Endowments for the Arts has recognized Burbank Senior Artists Colony as a model for creative aging.

For university alumni: Retirement housing on or near college campuses gives retirees the opportunity to avail themselves of the entire campus and its varied slate of activities, from athletic games to concerts to lectures. There are senior facilities near Notre Dame, Stanford, Duke, and UCLA (Belmont Village of Westwood). It is estimated that today eighty university-based communities are the drawing boards.

For gay and lesbian seniors: There are several complexes around the country, including Triangle Square in Hollywood, upscale versions in Santa Fe, New Mexico, and planned facilities are in Palm Springs, Vancouver, British Columbia, and across the country from Washington State to Florida.

RVers: For those RVers who are too tired or old to drive a mobile home, there are assisted facilities that help residents who can no longer travel.

The Rainbow's End RV Park in Livingston, Texas, assists residents in a caring environment.

For decades, there have always been groups looking out for others in their own community. There are senior complexes for groups identified by religion and ethnicity. One of the most unusual senior complexes is the Nikkei Senior Gardens in the San Fernando Valley. Populated by a strong and vibrant Japanese American community, seniors solidify relationships over common interests, such as gardening, horticulture, architecture, and Japanese dance and music. The community is open to all who are interested in an earthbound, organic, and Zen-like environment.

Today, boomers are worried that they will outlive their money. Those who converted from blue-chip stocks to annuities or low-risk investments might be okay. Others will have to make life-changing choices with their disposable incomes. The good news is that we have a world of resources at our disposal, and our decisions can be informed so that our needs will be met.

LIVING LA VIDA LOCA

At this moment, I know I will not stop teaching yoga. I know instinctively that I will continue to teach privately and at the university because my yoga students are so inspiring and energetic that I don't want to miss a day being in their presence. Maybe there will be something unexpected that will materialize outside of teaching. Of course, I'll still dance tango whenever I can. I'll visit my family and spend more time with my grandchildren and my mother. So my life is up in the air in terms of getting out of Dodge; on the other hand, maybe I don't want to leave Dodge. In the meantime, I can fantasize about faraway places to visit.

Since I have traveled quite a bit in my life, I now look for travel to make a difference. I have been going to Buenos Aires to dance tango for well over ten years. This year, I decided to change my routine travel plans. I went to Costa Rica for a week's yoga retreat and spent another week on an eco adventure. It was the best decision I have made in years.

Travel with some adventurous activity is now what I am looking for, and I found a compact travel company that suits my needs. I was looking for a trip to southern Spain that crossed over to northern Morocco, and I stumbled onto GAP Adventure Tours, a Canadian tour company. My trip this summer was exciting and invigorating. They have other tours that I'm excited to take, and I will go to Bali this summer and visit an old friend, and maybe it'll be Africa next year and Katmandu someday. The focus of my travel dreams provides a creative outlet for expressing myself with all my eccentricities in full bloom.

I have been amazed that there have been so many avenues to walk through in my sixties. Once I let go of unrealized expectations and fear of encountering change, I see infinite possibilities. I have not had too many irrational fears along the way, probably because I believe I am trying to visualize a fuller life. There is never any question that I might get bored, that I might insulate myself from friends, that I might strictly adhere to a routine that will calcify me, that I might be frightened to alter my lifestyle. I am more in tune with my needs and desires, more aware of my authentic and eccentric self, more able to corral my energy into productive and purposeful activities; and that is, once and for all, a blessing.

Text message from philosopher, physician, and humanitarian Albert Schweitzer (1875–1962)
late on 3rd day
now sun setting
moving thru herd of hippopotamuses
flash upon my mind
unforeseen & unsought,
the phrase, "reverence for life"

CHAPTER 13
CONVERSATIONS WITH MYSELF

Stay as you are wherever you are.

*If you do this instantly you will know
that you are what you have searched for,
for millions of years.*

*There is no search
because search is only for the lost.
But when nothing is lost
there is no meaning
to searching for an object.*

*Here simply Keep Quiet
Don't stir a thought from the mind,
Then you will know
Who you really Are.*

—Sri H.W.L. Poonja

ASHES TO ASHES

Last week, I met David's daughters, Janine and Camille, on the Santa Monica Pier at six o'clock in the evening. The skyline was a most beautiful sight. The sun was languishing in the orange sky tinged with pink. The white sand glittered, the azure sky sparkled, the waves danced spritely on their way to the shoreline. The girls were waiting for me with excitement. I ran to them at the apex of the pier; and there, standing on the lawn, we hugged each other tightly. I was introduced to Janine's husband, and as I shook his hand, I noticed Eric was carrying a shopping bag from an upscale store. My heart sank. I knew we were gathering on the pier to disperse David's ashes; but I choked up at the reality that in a simple rectangular box, in that very trendy shopping bag, were the remains of a life well lived.

I hadn't seen the girls for so long, and I missed them. They are splendid examples of David's best qualities, his ironic sense of humor and his absurdist view of life. They are bright and creative women in whose company I feel very special. Camille is also a very famous artist who shows her paintings in galleries all over the world. You'd never know from her humble demeanor and exotic beauty that many famous people collect her art. She just finished illustrating the newly released Alice in Wonderland to great acclaim. Her simplicity and grace is astounding. Janine, a talented teacher, is centered, funny, warm, curious, and happily married to a young man with her sensibilities and possibilities. The girls and their husbands live in the very northern part of California near the Oregon border. Small towns suit these two sisters and their mates. They are archetypes of the pioneer women in the 1800s that traveled west in covered wagons from the Mississippi River to find a new life and new opportunities. I would have jumped at the chance to head west from Missouri with Camille and Janine to chart a new life. Janine would be the driver; and Camille would entertain us all with her funny stories, her skewed sense of humor, and her artistic sensibility.

We walked down to the end of the pier telling stories about David, and we quickly realized that none of the stories we were telling about David were similar. Halfway down the boardwalk, we started laughing. It seemed David was one of those eccentric people who told different versions about his life to different people without concern as to their veracity. It wasn't so much that he was lying about his life but maybe romanticizing the truth.

I was stunned when Camille told me David never went to Berkeley. His ex-wife and sister said he only took a correspondence course. How could that be? David and I bonded over Berkeley in the sixties. He was on a football scholarship. He was a backup quarterback to Joe Kapp. When he was a junior, David left the political science department to study sculpture at the Art Institute of California in San Francisco. His ex-wife said he enrolled in the art institute but never graduated.

What was truth? What was fiction? He told me the story about how he was recruited into the CIA. He was living with two lesbians at the time, more like bisexual lesbians, and studying to be a sculptor. A recruiter knocked on his apartment door in Oakland. The recruiter said his political science professor recommended him as a prospective CIA agent. David's ex-wife told a very different story. He and his ex were living in Lima, Peru, working for the Peace Corps. I never knew David was in the Peace Corps. And married? And suddenly, he disappeared to Argentina. I knew he went to Argentina for R & R, but it appeared his narrative was more suited to his wild imagination than to the actual facts. There was no doubt that David was a superb raconteur.

EXT. SANTA MONICA PIER – EVENING
JOAN, JANINE, CAMILLE, and ERIC are halfway down the boardwalk, huddling together.

> CAMILLE
> (to Joan)
> You were the one who told me about Dad being in the CIA. He never told me if it was true until I asked him last year.

JOAN
I told you that years ago. Why did you wait so long to ask him?

CAMILLE
I was scared to ask him. Why didn't he tell me? Why was he was so secretive?

JOAN
I never knew he was in the Peace Corps. He told me a CIA recruiter showed up at his door. He had nothing better to do so he went to CIA headquarters in Langley, took a battery of tests, flew to Puerto Rico to jump out of planes and trained as a CIA agent.

JANINE
He jumped ...? What else did he do?

JOAN
He went to the Monterey Language Institute to learn Quechua because he went undercover in the Andes. He was tracking Che.

JANINE
Gee, this is really weird. Why didn't Mom tell us this stuff?

CAMILLE
I don't think Mom knew anything

    about Dad either. How long was
    he in South America?

       JOAN
    Four years. Until the North Kore-
    ans put a price on his head.

      CAMILLE
    He told me about Che, but did
    he really hunt Nazis and Dr.
    Mengele?

       JANINE
    Mom doesn't know that. Did you
    you know that?

       JOAN
    Yeah. We wrote a script about the
    last days of Che Guevara.

       JANINE
    But was it true?

  I didn't care if any of it was true or not true. It didn't matter to me if he elaborated on his life to others or if he simply wanted to forget whatever truth existed in his puzzling life. He was just David, and the rest was unimportant because he watched over my family and took care of me and loved us all even in the most difficult times. He had something special inside of him that only truly conscious and creative people have; the real story about David was not in the details.
  We walked to the end of the pier where a rather shabby-looking restaurant is located. We chose to gather on the least busy side of the pier, out of sight from people who could see what we were doing. Eric took the box of ashes out of the bag and handed it to me.

"It's really heavy," I said sadly.

"I never imagined ...," Janine trailed off. "I couldn't believe it when I picked it up ... how heavy it was," she continued in a flat tone.

We all stared in silence. Camille looked around to see if anyone was watching.

"I have a permit to do this, but it's for a boat," Camille whispered.

I thought a boat would be too much, and none of us had the will to go to that effort. David would have thought it over the top anyway. He always told me that if he got the big C, he wanted to get in a boat, go out into the ocean, and end it. David was a Zen kind of guy, and that meant he would embrace his universe and wait patiently for his last breath. He always said that when you die, the movie is over. He hated epilogues.

And then, it became *The Big Lebowski* moment. As I started to tip the plastic bag over the railing and into the ocean, the wind blew the ashes back into our faces.

"Blasted!" I said way too loudly. "This isn't working. I've got ashes all over me. I thought there was no wind."

"Let's go under the pier." Camille chuckled, saying, "This really is *The Big Lebowski!* Dad would love this."

We had gathered a bit of interest from a few restaurant workers who were taking a smoking break out the back door, so we walked quickly along the boardwalk to the stairs, which led to the beach. We took off our shoes and trudged on the cool black sand, circling back under the pier.

"Want some ashes, Joan?" Camille asked. I froze for a moment. I really wanted to remember David fully intact.

"I don't think so. You and Janine take your dad out into the ocean. It's low tide, so you can wade pretty far out."

And they did, side by side, Janine and Camille walked their father quietly out to sea, just the way he wanted his movie to end.

BECOMING ON BECOMING

It was a profound moment for us all. David was so big in our lives, and his presence will live on in each of us. When I dream about David, he is always standing on the sidelines—watching, observing, connecting to me with his penetrating dark eyes, a man with a Mona Lisa smile. I'm walking in his shoes most of the time these days. Whenever I visit my mother in Las Vegas, I think of David. He and my mother got along famously. When he died, I decided to tell her, but I wasn't sure she would remember him.

"David died, Mom." She looked up at me a little surprised. It took a moment to sink in.

"No," she whispered. "I really liked that guy."

"David said you were going to outlive him, Mom," I said to her. She laughed. "I did, didn't I?"

"You sure did," I replied.

These days, my mother looks radiant. She stays in her bed, sleeps, watches movies on TMC; but rarely does she understand what is going on. She only leaves the bed to go the bathroom or to the kitchen for a meal. She moves slowly on her walker; her spine is so round she cannot stand up. The squeaky noise of the walker sounds like nails on a blackboard. She is adamant that her hair is always neat, cut in a bob like Louise Brooks, the 1920s movie star; and her toes and nails painted her favorite color red. She alternates Chinese pajama sets that she once sewed herself—one in pink, the other in marigold. She looks elegant, stylish, and very much my mom.

She was named Ester at her birth in 1911, but her aunt changed her name to Estelle. Stella by Starlight, my father used to call her. "Isn't she beautiful?" he said to me whenever my mother came into a room. I called her the queen, la reina. She was Mrs. Las Vegas Senior Queen, Mrs. Senior Aerobics Instructor, Mrs. Executive Builder, devoted wife and mother. Estelle will keep my brother and me close for as long as she can, until she decides she is too tired to stay alive or until the party is over for her.

I watch her tenaciously cling to her life in her beautiful home, attended to by her son and her caretakers. Her eyes light up when I enter her small cloister. I know she has lived a full and rich life; and she deserves my love, honor, and respect. I never end a conversation without saying "I love you, Mommy" because she has been my guide in life and a role model for growing older.

My father died eight years ago, but I lost my father years before to progressive alcoholism. About the time I was thirty, my father was no longer responsive to anything but his generic vodka bottle hidden under the bathroom sink. I think he got a kick out of the idea that his social security check kept him in booze. When I left home at seventeen, my father seemed to know that his responsibility to his family was pretty much over. Who knows what my father would have evolved into if my mother had not taken over his world and allowed him to live his life on his own terms? On the other hand, my father had the black Irish in him, and those Irish love their drink.

In the last year of my father's life, I became mostly persona non grata. The last time I saw my father, he said some pretty negative things to me, and we didn't talk again. I tried to call him once, and he tried to call me back. And then he died. Maybe we forgave each other in a virtual world.

I wonder why I never called him back after that. It may be that I was afraid to hear his alcoholic slur on the phone. I was afraid to encounter more of the same sadness if I heard his voice again. I preferred to remember him at his best when he was my daddy growing up, when we traveled around the world, when he gave me history lessons, when we talked politics at dinner, when we gardened together on the hillside around our house, when he drove me to school and we listened to Don McNeill's Breakfast Club, when we went to mass at St. Raphael's together on Sundays, when he walked me down the aisle to get married, when he embraced David, when he loved my mother so very much that he couldn't help himself.

My mother said everything was going to be all right between my father and me. We forget things quickly in our family because, as in all families, we didn't want to address the underlying, endemic dysfunction. My mother said therapy was the worst thing that ever happened to people. It caused more trouble and solved nothing.

"We're just family, and we'll get over it," she said defensively.

I have often read that the death of a parent is a rite of passage, a time to carry the mantle of the adult orphan. In particular, if the death of a parent occurs in our sixties, we are set free and have the opportunity to recognize the true potential of self. If we have not already fully recognized our true potential, the death of a parent can be an inspirational time because we are allowed to examine our parent's emotional legacies. When a parent dies, it might be time to break old patterns of thoughts and feelings or keep ideals and sentiments that will be valuable for our own inner growth. It is a time to become ourselves.

I am now an orphan, and I have been set free.

MY MOTHER, MYSELF

On December 15, 2009, my mother died. She passed peacefully in her sleep in her home. She felt lucky to have been cared for with love and respect. My mother will always live within my heart and soul.

UNO

There is only one,
One mother always
So near to my soul.

There is only one,
One mother that
Shines so brightly
In my mind and heart.

Stella, Stella by Starlight

Some say with a smile.
True enough, she was
A unique and daring woman
Clad in diamonds and pearls
With sparkling dark eyes
And once-black braided hair.

Like Frida, my heroine,
She braved the world
With terms she defined,
Defiled by no one.
She forged through life
With rigors of discipline,
Knowing who she was,
What tone to set,
And whom to love.

And love she did,
Mythlike, spiderlike,
She clung to family
To model our journeys
With ecumenical steps,
Embracing forgiveness.

Constant and true,
One mother I cherish
In perpetuity with gratitude
For the plenty she gave me,
For my life, myself, my joy.

The Buddhists say that death is a continuation of life's journey. In the Hindu belief, the intonation of om or aum is the symbol of the absolute—the merging of past, present, and future, the manifest and the unmanifest in one form; hence, there is no difference between life and death. My mother's body is gone, but her soul, her energy now exists in the continuum of the universe. In death, her life continues, not in material form, but in a spiritual divineness.

I frequently call on her energy, and I hear her voice in my mind. She guides me, like David, like my father. I now am able to feel comforted by death, knowing that my soul will never die.

THINKING OUTSIDE THE MAT
Truth is given, not to be contemplated, but to be done.
Life is an action, not a thought.

—*F. W. Robertson,*
19th century English preacher

My mother lived her life following the true intent behind F. W. Robertson's quote. Rarely did my mother talk about doing something; she performed her role without fuss or fanfare. Rarely did anything distract my mother from doing the daily tasks that lay before her. She was intention-driven more than goal-oriented, and her achievements in life were many. And she showed me by example that life is an action not to be contemplated but to be done.

However, in order to know what action to take, contemplation is necessary. I need clarity before I know what to do. When I am practicing yoga on my mat, I am uniquely in my universe. I am practicing staying quiet in my mind and body; therefore, yoga prepares me for action that has truthful intention. In yoga, while I'm on my mat, there is no self-judging, no labeling, no distractions.

Life off my mat, however, looks different. I live on a continuum of self-judging, labeling, and distractions that render me unconscious. Of course, there are good distractions; for example, the beauty of a starry night, laughter from my grandsons, the fluidity of the ocean's waves. On the other hand, the unconscious distractions like people, places, and things prevent me from staying present.

"Without consciousness, things go less well," wrote Jung.

Distractions and habitual OCD behavior can feel oddly comforting. When I repeatedly go back and forth with my distractions, checking and rechecking small behaviors, playing and replaying my mind tapes, I go under the conscious radar and into avoidance mode. When I find myself reading multiple viewpoints on news and cultural events and checking out Hollywood celebrity stories that are pulp and fodder for mass distraction, I feel like I have been eating popcorn with butter minus any nutritional value plus the added fat. Distractions keep me in the shadow world, in my cave where light is obscured.

No prisons are more confining than the ones we know not ware in.
—Shakespeare, Twelfth Night

My list of daily distractions include the following:

Worrying

Doing more chores than necessary

Overly caring and managing children and/or elderly parents

Working too much

Excessively replaying our mental tapes from the past or future fantasies

Reading too much on the Internet, newspapers

Other distractions include the following:

Excessive complaining about physical pain

Going to the doctor frequently

Complaining about others

Watching too much TV, watching YouTube, reading blogs

I find it helpful to know what toxins I'm keeping alive and well within myself. If I am aware of the behaviors that are keeping me in the dark, I might be able to reduce the amount of time I get involved with other people's lives and find more time to create space for personal contemplation. I may have the opportunity to put more effort into healthy relationships, as opposed to dependent relationships, and in to more creative activities, as opposed to habitual self-destructive activities.

It is virtually impossible to make changes when residing in the dark places of the mind, not moving toward truth and light. The interior monologue turns into a litany of denials about how I am avoiding my feelings and emotions and not doing my inner work. The only way to make informed changes in life is to be truly conscious, present, and relaxed.

The following is my checklist regarding how to make changes:

Identify the change and work to change in the present moment.

Enlist the support of friends and family.

Encourage nonjudgment.

Look inside for signs and feelings, thoughts, and body language.

Make the intention to block negative thoughts.

Breathe.

Create alternative ways to change habitual states of negativity.

Rejoice at the small changes.

Practice compassion with setbacks.

Practice mindful awareness.

Mindfulness is a powerful technique that allows me the ability to move from the unconscious to the conscious. What is thrilling about living a conscious life is the possibility that I can stop my negative impulses, those reactive bits and pieces of behavior. I am giving myself the opportunity to shift focus to another level where inner beauty and power reside. I continually need to remind myself that everything I do to advance enlightenment is all good.

I FEEL PRETTY, OH SO PRETTY, I FEEL PRETTY AND WITTY AND WISE

I just met a man who made me feel beautiful—not just on the outside, but also, more importantly, on the inside. It was so very nice to have a man recognize my seasoned womanhood. And of all places, this happened at a tango festival.

The evening was winding down for me, and I wanted to have a glass of wine at the bar. It was my second *milonga* of the day, and I had danced my feet numb in my three-inch tango shoes. I was fumbling in my purse for money, and instinctively, I just happened to look up. I recognized the man who was dressed in black and was staring at me with piercing, sexy eyes. I devilishly put on my best Lauren Bacall sultry look and sashayed over to him with my best Lauren Bacall imitation.

INT. LOBBY OF THE MASONIC LODGE - NIGHT

JOAN walks over to a sexy man in his sixties.

       JOAN
 I know you.

       GRANT
 Yes, you do. And I know you.

JOAN
Last year.

GRANT
Yes, it was.

JOAN
You didn't call me.

GRANT
I lost your card.

JOAN
I ripped up your card two months after we met.

GRANT
I'm sorry. But I went to your milonga in LA when I was in town, and it was closed.

JOAN
On Saturday night? Impossible. You must have been there on Sunday night.

GRANT
I don't remember. I thought about you, though. You're a hard woman to forget.

JOAN
I'm just going to get a glass of wine. Can I buy you a drink?

GRANT
No, I'll buy you a drink. Do you remember my name?

JOAN
No.

GRANT
(smiles)
Grant.

An hour later, Grant and I were still talking. We both remembered each other, except for our names. It didn't seem to matter. What's in a name? We picked up the conversation we left off the previous year. He still couldn't find a mate, a companion to fulfill his life. All the women were too independent and weren't interested in coupling. He was frustrated and concerned that he wouldn't find a woman, but nonetheless, he was optimistic.

"And you? What about you? Have you found anyone?" he asked.

"No," I replied. "At the moment, I'm perfectly content to be myself."

For the first time in my life, I believed that I could actually live without a man, that being in my own skin seemed as natural as dancing tango. I had thrown away the mental crutches.

"Too bad," he responded blandly.

"Not so, Grant. It's all good."

"But I'm sixty-eight, and then I'll be seventy, and then what?" he pined.

"Maybe you should consider getting over the age thing and focus on all the gifts you have in your life."

Grant stared at me and finally said, "What a concept!"

For the last five years, I was revitalizing and renewing my sentient being; and I felt terrific talking to Grant about my life, my feelings, and the clarity of my path. I found Grant to be an intelligent, funny, handsome, sexy, thoroughly personal, and professional man who still actively works and creates his life. He was not threatened by my energy or my accomplishments. He too had pursued his passions of music, art, design, and tango; and we understood that we were mirroring each other in interests and cultural sensibilities.

And I felt pretty, oh so pretty.

I'M BEGINNING TO FEEL MY EARS: PLASTIC SURGERY AND OTHER CURES

Sometimes I don't feel so pretty, oh so pretty, and I don't feel so wise. I want the quick fix. I feel drab, oh so drab. So, is it really possible to work on my spiritual self and, at the same time, attend to my outer self? Of course! And I can attend to both gardens in small ways or take bold strokes. It's all a matter of desire and disposable income. I remember my mother saving for the rainy day when she would get her one and only face-lift. I think she was sixty, and she looked beautiful, like she had a great vacation.

It is inevitable that the sixtyish woman, or even man, considers the prospect of plastic surgery; to have or not to have, that is the question—whether 'tis nobler in the body to suffer the slings and arrows of facial and neck wrinkles or to take up arms against a ravaged visage and hunker down to the plastic surgeon's office and end the agony. However, if one lives in the 90210 zip code, the plastic surgery decision has been decided before anyone ever turns sixty. It's called the collective unconscious.

If a person has contemplated plastic surgery for the first time, the decision can be brutal to the psyche and ego, to say nothing of friends who get bombarded with "Should I do it? Do you think I need it?" Cost is the biggest obstacle. The good news is that there are many procedures available today to rejuvenate the skin or minor facial procedures with a local anesthetic at a variety of costs. Money does not have to be an impediment if someone really wants to pep up the face. Besides, it feels good to resurface.

I do not judge anyone for submitting to plastic surgery or any other facial treatment. I have friends who have had Fraxel, photo facials, cheek lifts, eye lifts, laser treatments, acid peels, nose jobs, boob jobs, liposuction; and the list goes on. One of my friends, Dr. Cynthia Boxrud, ophthalmologist/plastic surgeon from the neck up, is one of the top surgeons in Los Angeles. I'm really lucky because I get the best advice about perking up the facial landscape. Cynthia does not like to give full face-lifts or cut when other noninvasive procedures are available.

"No one wants to look pulled or plastic anymore," Cynthia told me one day when I was in for Botox.

Rarely does anyone speak of having "work done." If one looks like he or she had a good rest instead of looking like a car ran over his or her face, if facial muscles move without contorting, there is no need for a jarring outcome. I admit living in Los Angeles, one of the capital cities of plastic surgery, has a cult of glamour. Beauty is ubiquitous in my alternative universe. The superficial is revered and inner beauty set aside for pseudoconversations about how great that last yoga retreat was on Maui. Didn't you think the yoga instructor was so hot? Are you going to Cabo next April with him? Inner work is hyped to fit the cultural tone of the moment. No one really takes yoga retreats seriously.

When a woman begins to feel her ears after her partial face-lift begins to heal, she looks for the next new procedure. The problem is that these physical alterations take the focus off the intention to nurture the soul. But, hey, get the Botox or a cheek lift if it feels good. No judging, please. Then get back to inner work.

DON'T BELIEVE EVERYTHING YOU THINK
Below is one of my favorite quotes comes from Alfred D. Souza, writer/philosopher from Brisbane, Australia:

For a long time, it had seemed to me that life was about to begin—real life. But there was always some obstacle in the way, something to be gotten through first, some unfinished business, time still to be served, and a debt to be paid. Then life would begin. At last, it dawned on me that these obstacles were my life. Happiness is the way. So, treasure every moment that you have. And treasure it more because you shared it with someone special, special enough to spend your time, and remember that time waits for no one.

So stop waiting

until you finish school,
until you lose ten pounds,
until you gain ten pounds,
until you have kids,
until your kids leave the house,
until you start work,
until you retire,
until you get married,
until you get divorced,
until Friday night,
until Sunday morning,
until you get a new car or home,
until your car or home is paid off,
until spring,
until summer,
until fall,
until winter,
until you are off welfare,
until the first or the fifteenth,
until your song comes on,
until you've had a drink
until you've sobered up,
until you die,
until you are born again

to decide that there is no better time
than right now to be happy.

It's not a tall order to be happy; in fact, it's relatively easy to be happy and joyful most of the time. The only caveat—and this is a big caveat—is to eliminate the majority of our negative thinking.

In an article in the *Sentient Development Speculations* on the future of intelligent life, the National Science Foundation estimated that people have, on average, fifty thousand daily thoughts and sometimes upward of sixty thousand. Most of these thoughts are pure nonsense, and about one thought per second during every waking hour is negative; that translates into about 70 to 80 percent negative thoughts. What is more startling is that 95 percent are the same thoughts we had yesterday and the day before and the day before that! You can imagine how a daily barrage of negative thoughts can sabotage our psyches, stunting our mental growth and causing bitterness, stress, anxiety, disappointment, and depression. Most of the negative thoughts circle around making mistakes, battling guilt, planning ahead, worrying, fantasizing, and drifting. A minuscule number of thoughts focus on the present.

However hard we try to obliterate our negative thinking, it simply gets the better of us because negative thoughts register more deeply than positive ones. I have the best intentions to stay positive despite my hardwiring to be negative; and yet, my first response is negative, deflecting criticism of others, turning situations catastrophic, anticipating harsh words, or polarizing emotions with classic good/bad conflicts. I want to find better coping skills so I can dig for the positive and avoid warring with myself for the rest of my time on this earth.

I was speaking to one of my recovery clients one afternoon. She had suffered past trauma, and it had been one of the major causes for her alcoholism. She was angry with herself for her addiction, and she was angry that she let her past defects permeate the present. She was full of negative thinking.

I suggested that because she was so frequently challenged by negative thoughts, she might be more conscious of any happy thoughts that came up and embrace these happy thoughts as truthful moments. With more focus on relaxation, breathing, exercise, a healthy diet, and moderate eating, my client's self-talk would be less negative and more informed by her present environment.

I also suggested that she focus on her relationship with her daughter and avoid reactive behavior in the recovery house. Her pure mother love was a source of pride and joy. By nurturing her primary relationship with her daughter, in time, she would increase her happiness quotient. I encouraged her to continue her commitment to exercising, which boosted her adrenaline and reduced her cortisol and epinephrine levels, thereby reducing stress and anxiety.

The following is my checklist for staying positive:

I check myself periodically for negative self-talk.

I humor during my waking hours and smile every time I think of it.

I keep a healthy lifestyle.

I surround myself with positive people.

Everyone benefits from a healthy personal relationship. Both women and men have bonding hormones. Research shows that women's brains respond to a loving relationship by releasing a hormone called oxytocin, the bonding hormone, which calms and reduces stress. When women bond either with other women or family, they generate acceptance and appreciation, which helps to foster personal happiness. Men's bonding hormone is called vasopressin. Not all men have equal levels of this hormone; however, increases in vasopressin can come from more frequent physical contact with a woman, a wife or a companion.

It's difficult to be negative about the benefits of being happy. It's a relief to know that I do not have to hold on to self-sabotaging negative thinking, and I can devote more time to inner peace and tranquility. I can be happy gazing at a starry sky or watching the sun rise in the desert or set over the ocean; I can admire a full moon, watch children play, and embrace the love inside myself. I can think of a hundred ways to feel happy.

My happiness list includes the following:

My family, especially my grandsons

My mother's eyes

Teaching yoga/practicing yoga, especially yin yoga
Dancing Argentine tango

Meditation

Breathing

Irony

A beautiful fall morning

UCLA campus

My supervisor at the Wooden Center

My yoga students

My 6 pm yoga class on Tuesdays/Thursdays

My favorite exercise machine at the Wooden Center (for the butt)

Friday Shabbat services at Jordan's temple school

A glass of red wine at dinner

A nonfat vanilla latte

My favorite jeans

Slow hands

    I realize that happiness is relative, and there are degrees of happy feelings throughout a day. Moods change as situations change. If I don't get a call from someone I am expecting to call, who said he would call, my mood can turn negative. Sometimes I'm vaguely at peace; other times, I feel over-the-top blissful. And there are times in my life when I am in balance and know exactly what to do to make me joyful; other times, I remain calm in the face of adversity or panic or just plain frustration and just sit with the feelings. Then, there are other times when I don't maintain my composure, like wigging out when my computer doesn't work or losing all patience when I drive in Los Angeles traffic.

That moment of the all-powerful negativism inhabiting my body and mind is the exact moment that the source of my happiness is lost. When that happens, I reconnect to the present and focus on what makes me happy, and I smile.

I FEEL THE EARTH MOVE

I had a moment in the shower this morning when I found my mind, God forbid, grasping for a man! I admonished myself and choked on my mantra: *I am enough for myself, I am enough for myself.* I said it over and over again until I reconnected with the present. I got out of the shower, stood with my towel tightly wrapped around me, and tried to quiet my mind. My first instinct was to go on a yoga retreat immediately, get away from my routine, my mental loop of neediness, and energize my present. I couldn't go on a retreat, but I remembered what it was like when I spent five days in silence and how glorious it was for my soul. I had nowhere to go and nowhere to hide, and I allowed myself to struggle to let go of the old thinking and to create more inner space to embrace my joy.

I began to breathe deeply to find stillness, and I recognized that my emotions were a direct communication from my inner self, my soul. I thought of Carole King and felt the earth move under my feet. It actually felt good to feel the loneliness and the discomfort of embracing my emotions and not assign blame. My body began to physically let go, and as my sense of honor returned, negative thoughts turned into positive self-reinforcements.

Recently, a new book title caught my eye: *Loneliness As a Way of Life.* I approached the book with trepidation. Who wants to read about loneliness? The author, Thomas Dumm, writes that this modern-world loneliness may be the way; but readers should not shy away from that state. Loneliness gives us autonomy and the ability to make decisions on our own terms. It may be painful, but loneliness can make us more rational and self-aware. Paradoxically, loneliness may also lead us to embrace the community of others, connecting the innermost to the outermost.

However, the flip side of the freedom we attain with loneliness is that we still and forever will live in a fragmented society, and our human condition can be an impediment to our relations with others. Dumm writes about the many distractions in our world that can separate us from others and inhibit our need to self-examine who we truly are.

The most terrifying thing is to accept oneself completely.
—*Carl Jung*

Acceptance is a burden and a challenge we all face, and it is uniquely our own journey.

Text message from Chinese royal Hong-Shi (1704–1727)
when zen practice
is completely developed,
there is no center,
no extremes;
there r no edges or corners
it's perfectly round, frictionless

CHAPTER 14
CALM TO THE CORE

I love to dance. Dancing energizes my soul and infuses my body with rhythm. When I discovered tango, it was the most compatible aesthetic for my natural set of skills. When I heard tango music and saw the dance, all I wanted to do was immerse myself in its rhythms and melodies with my body and mind. I followed my instincts and sought out my passion and have never regretted it since my initial discovery of the music and the dance. I've met dancers from all over the world, experienced the charms of a few Argentine lovers, had so many adventures I cannot count them all, explored cities I never would have thought of going to, and found a world that was as passionate as I was about Argentine tango.

My friend Valdimir Estrin has written many poetic observations about Argentine tango, and his words have always resonated with me.

> *Tango enters your life as a simple interest, develops into a nice hobby, slowly grows into an obsession ... and gradually becomes your lifestyle ... tango is a bouquet of human emotions –passion, anger, happiness, desire, lust, jealousy, love ... interpreted uniquely by each individual person ... expressed on the dance floor. Tango always allows you to communicate your feelings and emotions much stronger ... you are happy, you dance one way; you are sad, you dance another way. No tango is every the same. Every dance is unique because tango is impro-*

visational. You may know the steps in your head, but your heart tells you where to move.

    Tango is my joy, my habit, my Zen, the place that feels more like home than anywhere except my yoga mat. It is a pathway to self-mastery, to simpatico with others, to wordless conversation—instant nods that lead me to dance with strangers and not feel the need to share the details of my life. Tango is in my skin; its sensations, its smells, its emotions run through my body and cause me to breathe. There is no struggle in tango; there is no drama. There is only the melting of two bodies dancing to the language of tango music.

    Tango brings people together from all walks of life. Age does not exist because tango is timeless. It does not matter who you are or what you do. It only matters that you dance tango. Tango spans decades, continents, nations, and people. Tango is a culture unto itself with a rich history and passionate mystery. With every tango played, the heart and soul succumb to its alluring charms, and tango dancers fall deeper in love with the dance.

    Argentine tango is unique to all other dances. It is the most intense lead-follow dance on the planet. The upper body remains still, motionless even, except for a very subtle directional movement with the shoulders and torso. Tango is danced primarily from the waist down. The woman does not know the next step. She must follow the man; it is the man who creates the space for the woman to follow him, and then the woman instinctively complies. Tango is always improvised when it is danced on the salon floor in a social setting because it is an intuitive conversation.

    Show tango is different. It is a performance involving choreography. It is showy, flashy, quick, sexy, provocative, and stylized. The dancers tell stories with staged precision. Stories are usually about lost love, jealously, possessiveness, and defending honor against the insults of others. Leave it to the Italian immigrants who came to Argentina to find work. The stories were in their hearts and minds.

    On the dance floor in a social setting, very little conversation takes place when two people dance tango. Appropriate courtesies and pleasantries are exchanged, but the real conversation takes place between the man and the woman through the contact of their bodies and the movement of their legs. It is a sensual and intimate connection, but for the magic to occur, both the man and the woman must be fully involved with the music. Tango music is the conduit through which the conversation takes place between dancers, so it becomes extremely important to have familiarity with and understanding of the musical context.

When I tell people I dance Argentine tango, they always ask me if I compete in dance contests because most people assume that tango is danced for competition. The confusion is a result of assuming Argentine tango and American tango are the same. American tango is part of the ballroom world within which there are many other types of dances. Argentine tango is specifically danced in salons called *milongas,* and it is rare that there ever would be a competition. Tango was originally conceived as a social dance, and framing it as a competition is antithetical to the intent of its origins.

IT TAKES TWO

I started taking tango lessons when I was in full menopause. That doesn't sound very exotic, but it mattered to me greatly since I was feeling a little low on estrogen. Through hot flashes and memory loss, I learned the basic steps and felt the music moving through my body. It was like falling in love over and over again.

When novice dancers first begin the basic mechanics of tango, they become obsessive and dance sometimes four to five times a week. The dance is challenging and complicated, and it takes time to become familiar with the canon of tango music. It's all a rush at the beginning, but it requires an abundance of patience and concentration to make a dent in the learning curve. A male novitiate watches the dancers on the floor for hours, sometimes never getting up the courage to ask a woman to dance for a year. But the woman anxiously waits to be asked no matter how new she is to the dance. At the same time it is important to sit as the man would do and watch at the *milongas* so that she could learn to be an expert follower and be able to dance with any male dancer. I watched for a very long time and avoided the nods to dance, which gave me the opportunity to gain familiarity with the music and the steps.

The first year I learned tango, I went to Buenos Aires. I was compelled to see for myself the city that produced the dance I fell in love with. Buenos Aires is the generator of the magical, mystical feeling that caused my passionate addiction. I learned the history of tango by dancing with the local men, visiting important landmarks, and talking with maestros and dancers. I've been back to Buenos Aires thirteen times to dance. Except for my first trip, I rarely experienced the surrounding metropolis because I only haunted the salons del tango at night and then slept until noon. I usually danced about six or seven hours a day. Sometimes I took a week of intensive classes with a master teacher I wanted to study with in order to refine a particular dance movement. In the off hours, I searched for the perfect tango shoes or met up with Argentine friends or people I knew from the States.

Over the years, I have had the privilege of taking tango lessons from most of the greatest tango maestros in the world—whether they were in Buenos Aires, Europe, or in the United States. These maestros and maestras were my mentors; and during the years of instruction, we became friends and were always happy to see each other when we met up, even when years had passed. A dancer never forgets a master teacher.

I am older now than when I started to dance tango, but not less passionate. I look around the *milongas* wherever I happen to be, and I see older men and women dancing with joy, and it gives me inspiration to continue my tango journey.

I am always thrilled when a man nods his head at me from across a crowded dance floor and beckons me to dance. I respond with a slight nod of my head and demurely rise out of my chair. My eyes follow his direction for several moments so I know where he wants to meet me on the dance floor. It is his choice, so I dutifully walk to meet him where he waits for me. We stand next to each other, listening for the music to begin. I know that an Argentine man will not dance immediately when the music starts because it is the custom to make sure he knows what tango is playing. I too wait to make sure I understand the music.

Then, as if by magic, we know we should begin to dance. He extends his left hand for me to take; and as tradition and dance convention play out, he puts his right arm around the middle of my back, and I put my left arm around his neck. This is our tango embrace, our moment of connection. The first step is so very important. I feel his body lead me to a side step to the right, which I actually take first, but it looks as if we are moving seamlessly. I patiently wait for the next move, which once again the man leads. When the tango music ends, we release our bodies from our embrace. It is our mutual acknowledgement that our dance conversation is over.

How well dancers know the music is how well one leads and follows. Our ears and body are instruments of knowledge in the tango world. We do not need words to translate this intimacy. We continue to dance two more tangos together. This is called a tanda—three tangos in succession by different composers, some perhaps sung by a famous tango singer. Or we may dance to a tango vals or to a *milonga,* which has a more folkloric rhythm, oftentimes with a rapidity that leaves us breathless. We leave each other with a "gracias" or "thank you" and walk back to our respective seats. And if we are fortunate, we understand intuitively that our tanda was an inspirational experience because we always remember the partner and the dance that took us into another universe.

> *If you gaze for long into the abyss, the abyss also gazes into you.*
> *—Nietzsche*

For over fifteen years, I have gazed into the world of tango, my abyss, and have found it to be one of the greatest gifts in my life, slightly behind my sons, grandsons, and yoga. I have the most respect for the dance and its influence on my life. It continues to be a transformative experience, adding grace and stillness to my life. It is also a heart-opening experience as it puts me in touch with people all over the world who love and appreciate tango.

I started out to make a documentary about tango once upon a time. It was called *Chasing the Tango,* and its premise was to capture, in real time, tango dancers around the world. For the past eighty years, Argentine tango has had a formative influence on those who have listened to tango music and have learned the dance. Tango is not just danced in Buenos Aires, where it originated, but also in Istanbul, Japan, China, Finland, Holland, Israel and almost in every country of the world. Since the 1980s, tango has undergone a metamorphosis created by a new generation of young Argentine men and women who began to carefully renurture, cherish, and preserve its traditions. Tango will live on and endure as long as there are dancers who passionately desire to tell its story.

BUT IT REALLY TAKES ONE

I alone am the only one that can make a difference in myself in the decade of my sixties. My personal belief does not belie all other philosophies for living a full, productive, and conscious life. However, it has been my preference and my joy to stay connected with myself through the practice of yoga. Yoga is also the way in which I express my physical and energetic sense of self. Through my practice I am more able to stay present, to live energetically, to stay internally balanced, and to enjoy good health through the principles of breath, alignment and movement.

I like to think that yoga is an aesthetic; it is a creative dance that blends movement and expression. When I'm practicing yoga, I feel like I'm the queen of disco, the sexy Latina dancer, the prima ballerina, and everything beautiful wrapped up inside me. No one is watching me, and no one is judging me. My mat is my universe. I am always amazed by what I learn daily about moving into a position without needing to get anywhere. From the flowing yoga movements come joy and renewal. I'm excited and enthusiastic to be alive and mindful of my being. New ideas often enter my mind as I breathe and flow. I let them go, knowing that they will return in time.

Yoga is derived from the Sanskrit word *yuj,* which means to "bring together" or "to unite." The practice integrates all aspects of the individual—body, mind and spirit—to bring about balance and harmony in a sentient being. There are three parts to a yoga practice: breathing, physical movement (or *asana*), and meditation.

Breathing is the linchpin of the practice, for it yokes the body and mind together. "Breath" in Sanskrit is prana, and it means "life force." Breath is sacred, and breathing is the major mechanism that inspires us to be present. Yoga breathing is deeper; it is called belly breathing, or bellows breathing. If we can watch our breath and find it interesting, as my master teacher Max indicated, then we are attending to our inner core, our spiritual nature.

I like to refer to the moving or physical component of a yoga practice as a "moving meditation" because it connects a clear mind with breath and physical movement. The movement component helps me to let go of my thoughts and to distance myself from the constant need to feed my ego, like a two-year-old who nags and pulls on his mother's leg with unrelenting force to gain attention. Yoga movements and postures do not require physical perfection; a yoga practice is about the release and openness of space in our body, space that gives us room to breathe and the ability to be still.

Bodies contain both matter and energy. Our internal energy is responsible for our emotional state, its moods and dispositions. Yoga gives me an awareness of how my energy centers, *chakras,* influence my behavior. It works like this: on my yoga mat, I have fewer distractions in my practice and I am able to still my energy and surrender to the moment; off the yoga mat, when I take my yoga mindset, I am bombarded by distractions and my stress and anxiety levels increase. However, because I practice yoga daily, I have more awareness about how my actions and emotions are affecting how I handle life's situations.

I am facilitated in creating more awareness in my life through the practice of meditation. The simple definition of "meditation" is to quiet the mind; yet, this definition doesn't necessarily mean that we should not think while we are meditating. Of course, we are going to have thoughts because we cannot on cue direct our mind to stop thinking. We have a thought every second or two! The problem is not with thinking per se, but with thinking that is "stuck" on one track or loop. Meditation helps relieve the need to push the mind into thinking non-stop on a continuum (and remember how many of our thoughts are negative). Scientists at the Ahmanson-Lovelace Brain Mapping center at UCLA tell us that when we relax the mind, we relax our body as well; hence, the value of meditation in the area of stress reduction.

Students always tell me how difficult it is to meditate. "I can't stop thinking," they say. So think; but when the thoughts come into the mind, detach from those thoughts, let them go, watch them pass in front of the mind. Wave them good-bye and smile. As master yogi Max said so eloquently, "Let the thoughts pass like clouds moving in front of your minds and simply watch as they go by."

But because we are so familiar, so comfortable with our thought patterns, we are reluctant to let go of them. We are very resistant when it comes to letting go of old wounds, irritations and jealousies because they are so much a part of the unconscious mind. Our struggle is a familiar backdrop to our present state of mind; in a strange, complicated way, struggle is soothing. Ultimately, however, that struggle we are addicted to produces anxiety and self-judgment.

Since thinking cannot totally be eliminated, the way to stay calm in a meditation practice is to find a good way to relax. There are many creative techniques that I use in meditation apart from watching my thoughts go by like clouds or watching my breathing.

I challenge my thoughts and ask myself if I have any suggestions for improving the meditation. I focus on breathing deeply, or I pay close attention to my posture, a straight spine. I hold and sustain contradictory thoughts; for example, if I have the desire to move because I'm tired of sitting with a straight back, I entertain the idea of not moving. I pay attention to ambient sounds in the room, imagine a beautiful scene on the beach, release, and relax every part of the body. I ask myself, what is it I really want in life? Or I muse on what I was like before I was born. Or better yet, I'll just check my mind at the door and get back to it later.

The good news is that brain mapping studies reveal that meditation increases happiness and reduces stress, which gives everyone a better quality of life. Long-term meditation is associated with increased gray matter, increased density of the brain stem, increased thickness of the spinal cord, increased blood flow, and improvement in cognitive learning. Why wouldn't we meditate?

I always hear my students remark as they are leaving class that they feel so much better, more energetic, and at the same time, more relaxed and much more positive. That is because a yoga practice focuses on the balance between the mind and body; it allows us to let go and surrender to the present moment.

The manner in which a yogi engages in the practice of yoga is through the selection of small intentions during a practice instead of on goals as in "I have to touch the floor; otherwise, I haven't executed the asana properly." The intention of moving into a pose with patience, grace and alignment allows me to stay in the present without grasping or forcing myself into position. If I take the intentional aspect of yoga off my mat and into my life as a replacement for the goal-oriented Western concept of pushing toward achievement, I can live my life with more ease and a deeper sense of purpose and joy. This is the essence of yoga: enjoying the journey and not heading for the destination.

There is a wonderful book written by one of my master yoga teachers, Steve Ross, called *Happy Yoga*. Eckhart Tolle, author of *The Power of Now*, comments about Happy Yoga that "underneath Steve's refreshing humor and light-heartedness lies an uncompromising dedication to spiritual truth and awakening." Steve's book is what one might call a nontraditional yoga book because it is not about alignment and perfectly executed positions. The book is about staying happy by distancing ourselves from our daily grind. Steve proffers that even though we cannot change the dynamics of our world, we can effect change in ourselves. In other words, we can follow the yogic way of life and its principles of an open heart and mind, and what follows will be our bliss.

Steve is probably referred to as an acquired taste in some yoga circles. Steve's classes are happy, full of alternative music, mixed with some cool world music. He prefers to teach in a kind of rock-and-roll atmosphere, packed with students in his twice-a-day classes at his studio.

"It gets them in the door of the yoga studio," he told our class one day. "They get jiggy with it, and it's all good."

Music is one of the key ingredients to practicing happy yoga as students lead themselves into their own brand of bliss. Steve uses humor to inspire, and an easy banter permeates the class. Students keep coming back for more, so he must truly be spreading the bliss.

One of my students, Justin, was so inspired by his yoga classes with me that he wrote an article for the UCLA *Total Wellness* magazine. The title of the piece was "Yoga: Rejuvenate Your Mind and Strengthen Your Body." Justin thinks that yoga is the new trend of physical and mental fitness for the twenty-first century. Stars do it, athletes do it, and sixty-year-olds do it. Justin quotes Ann Pizer, a yoga expert who lists some of the benefits of doing yoga, including the following:

Enhanced muscle tone

Stronger physical endurance

Improved sleep

Pain prevention

Mental calmness

Deeper breathing

Increased body awareness

Stress reduction

Increased immunity to disease

I would like to add physical balance to this list. Balance is a very important benefit of yoga, especially for the older population, the boomers in particular, and even older folks in their seventies and eighties. We lose balance as we age, and the loss of our balance prefigures an accident waiting to happen. A yoga practice of at least twice a week improves balance for anyone, especially for people in age-groups whose muscles have lost some mass. Yoga also strengthens mental awareness in conjunction with physical balance. At any age, muscle mass can be toned and expanded, and mental acuity can be strengthened.

There are about twenty-two kinds of yoga. Among them are gentle yoga, power yoga, hatha flow, ashtanga, anusara, kundalini, Iyengar, and yin yoga (stretching and meditation), which is my particular favorite. It is sensible to take an introductory class, try out teachers, and finally commit to a yoga practice by buying a mat.

On the first day of my yoga teacher training with Max, he asked each person in the class why he or she had signed up for the class. When Max asked me, I said, "Because I want to live forever." I am not sure if I was joking or not, but I do know that anyone who practices yoga will live life with greater joy.

FORGIVING IS A BITCH

It is only with the heart that one can see rightly; what is essential is invisible to the eye.
—*Antoine De Saint-Exupéry*

I meditate. I burn candles. I drink green tea. And I still want to smack someone who offends me.

It is challenging and completely exasperating to forgive someone. It might even be harder to forgive yourself for past offenses. It takes time to forgive those who are unrelentingly negative or unconscious in thought, word and deed. The sad truth is that people offend without realizing it because they are maddeningly unconscious. They harbor perceived insults, jealousies and offenses; sometimes their behavior can be passive-aggressive. And what's more offensive, some equal-opportunity offenders are injustice collectors who want to extract a pound of flesh for past or perceived offenses. I want to change these people, shake them up, turn them upside down and scream in their faces to wake up and connect themselves to the present. What I have to remember is that their discourteous behavior is not about me. If I was the problem, I could do something about it, but I can't because it is about the other person being unconsciousness.

Is anything unforgivable? Can I forgive those who perpetrated the 9/11 attacks on the World Trade Center or who systematically kill and starve the innocent around the world? Can I forgive an individual murderer who kills in an act of rage or premeditation? I am always in awe of a mother who forgives the killer of her son or daughter or husband. What grace, honor, and dignity she gives herself!

It is possible to separate the actual horrific acts from the perpetrators who are flawed and psychologically sick? I think it is possible, and I think it is difficult. But if I do not forgive others, I cannot forgive myself. I will keep my inner anger inside myself, and it will prevent me from living a truthful and honorable life. For me, the essence of forgiveness is a spiritual practice through which I can acquire clarity and stay close to my inner truth.

I remember when my heart was always closed around my ex-husband. My heart felt like it was in a vise every time he treated me with disdain and dismissed me. I felt rage and anger, and those feelings were locked inside my heart and tortured me from time to time. It exploded at my son's wedding. I walked out of the wedding reception filled with anger and resentment for him. And no one in my family understood because, why should they? They were only reacting to my discourteous act at a moment of celebration. The wedding flagged an unconscious lack of forgiveness.

With forgiveness, I am not a captive of my own anger. The Buddha said:

Hate never yet dispelled hate. Only love dispels hate.

I carry around some feelings of loss, the desire that I want things to be different, and this causes me discomfort. We all know people who were mean to us, who dropped us after the divorce, gossiped about us behind our back, told lies to those who liked us once upon a time, and those who stole time and money from us or robbed us of our reputations?

The text message to me from Hong-Shi is very clear and simple: He is saying that I can strive for no edges, no corners, and no extremes. My world can be perfectly frictionless and round if I so choose. This is the Zen of forgiveness. The people who wounded me or traumatized me are not me. When I forgive those who hurt me, I have the option of distancing myself from them in the present and the ability to let go of others in the past. It is also difficult to forget completely because there is personal loss, but the hurt and anger diminish with time.

Forgiveness is the most difficult and challenging state of being. Yet, forgiveness is integral to resolving issues, communicating more effectively, and providing empathy and understanding.

The key to forgiveness is to control the ego. The ego produces too much self-talk and creates defense mechanisms, which cause projections and justifications for behavior. Putting limits on the ego gives me opportunity to increase clarity, open my heart, and generate positive energy for my family and myself.

I teach yoga and meditation to vets at New Directions, an alcohol and drug treatment center on the grounds of the VA Hospital in West Los Angeles. My clients are very important to me. They are devoted yogi practitioners who show up every week to master their demons and find inner peace.

One day, a man—big, strong, intense—posed the question:

INT. REC ROOM, VA HOSPITAL - DAY

                   YOGI
      How do you forgive, Joan? I just
      can't forgive.

JOAN
You mean you can't forgive those you hurt you deeply in the past?

YOGI
I can't get them out of my mind. I think about it all the time.

JOAN
Forgiving is about opening your heart. Sometimes it might be a long journey. But inner peace is on the other side.

YOGI
How do you open your heart?

JOAN
Meditation is one way. The heart has healing energy.

YOGI
They did me wrong.

JOAN
Changing attitudes or behaviors takes time. It's done with intentions. One person, one wrong at a time.

Several weeks later ...

JOAN
How's it going with the forgiving?

>   YOGI
> It's okay. I feel a little better with
> my quiet mind. But those guys
> still get to me.
>
>   JOAN
> It takes time. Be patient.

And he was patient, and he is on the path of forgiveness, and he is beginning to recognize that there can be joy in his life.

I'M OVER IT

I turned sixty-six recently, and I'm over it already. My bone density is that of a thirty-five-year-old, and I'm collecting social security. It was a good birthday.

Last night at my usual Saturday *milonga,* my good friend Tito asked me if I was all right. He is a longtime tango friend, and he always asks me how I'm doing. He knows that I live alone, work hard, and try to do the right things in my life.

"How are you really?" Tito asked.

"Besides the fact that I'm sixty-six, I'm good. Let's dance," I prodded.

"How do you feel?" he persisted.

"I feel really good. I feel like I'm nineteen."

"Muy buen, Flaca. Bailmos."

Text message from my son Jonathan
mom bring costume 4 Halloween
trick o treating with boys

Text message from Mom
@ 66 I'm my own costume
love, moms

    I've worked through a few things in my life, covered some important ground, and found some real joy in being true to myself while I'm living alone. I love my family more than I can say. I've had the joy of David, a marriage that produced two beautiful young men and their offspring, gave back to my community, and made fabulous friends in my brief tour on planet Earth. Despite it all, even today, I'm still a girly girl still holding just a little bit of a fantasy that Prince Charming will find me. Hey, a girl can hope. But deep down inside my redundant mind, I know that wishful thinking is literally counterproductive to living a healthy and truthful existence.

    So every day of my life, probably more than once, I offer gratitude to the universe for all my gifts, all my joys, all my loves, and the many opportunities that have been given to me in my life. I'm truly blessed. Besides, I now can text-message.

    Boomers still have a path to walk and a journey to fulfill. Some say we were turncoats to our original dreams. We were consumed by the culture war that divided our generation; we have definitely squandered some of our golden years and the opportunities they provided because we took for granted what we were given for the past forty years. We lived high on the hog and failed to pay attention to the realities around us. Some might say we lost consciousness.

    Yet, I postulate that boomers are in an evolutionary stage. Sure, we took detours, found other routes, pacified ourselves, and self-gratified. We lied to ourselves and to our friends, but we also told some truths, and we are just now winding our way back home. Our task in life is to be conscious so that we can be grounded in who we are and how we want to live and love for the rest of our lives.

I know I'm lonely sometimes, but I am comforted in my loneliness. It is not so relevant anymore because I'm getting to know myself better each minute, each hour, each day. I'm happy and grateful in my sixties. I'm so over that number.

Life may not be the party we hoped for,
but while we're here,
we should dance
as if no one is watching.
Life isn't so short anymore.
We're living longer,
so let's all smile and laugh
as much as we can,
have no regrets,
love truly and passionately,
forgive quickly,
kiss slowly
and stay in the light of the power of now.

Who knows who wrote this poem. I found it in the bathroom of a dance studio after teaching a tango lesson. Does it really matter anyway?

We are here and it is now.
Further than that,
all human knowledge is moonshine.
—H. L. Mencken

EPILOGUE

It has been four years since I began to write *60, Sex & Tango, Confessions of a Beatnik Boomer.* The evolution of my journey after publishing my memoir has taken some interesting twists and turns. What is constant is that I still dance tango as if no one is watching, I still feel like I'm 19, I still feel that life is an awesome adventure, and I still follow my passions – they are the source of my finest moments and the essence of my soul. But something else quite wonderful and fulfilling entered my life.

In January 2010, I found myself attending a conference on keynote speakers sponsored by the National Speakers Association. True to my mantra of never planning career moves, I had no clear idea why I was at the conference except that it was held in Las Vegas, Nevada, and that is where my family lives – two adult sons and five grandchildren. The previous November I thought about what I was supposed to be doing with my life after my memoir was published. It occurred to me that there must be another adventure to follow. So, on a whim, I called the National Speakers Association in Tucson, AZ, and spoke to a woman by the name of Gemenie Babb. I remarked to Gemenie that her name was right out of a romance novel, and then I began to riff on what kind of woman with a name like Gemenie Babb might be doing in a story about love and lust. We laughed like high school girls. I told Gemenie that the reason for my call was that I thought I wanted to learn how to be a professional speaker. After all, I was a high school speaking champion. Surely that gave me some qualifications. Gemenie encouraged me to attend the Keynote Speakers conference in Las Vegas as a way to get introduced to the public speaking world and see its stars in action.

If nothing else, the trip to Las Vegas was an excuse to spend two days in the middle of the week with my family. And, if there was to be something more inspiring for me, well, so much the better.

I walked into a large room energized by a crowed of good-looking men and women. I fumbled my way into the one seat left in the middle of a long row, computer falling out of my arms, and sat next to three adorable women singers from the south. We became fast friends.

I heard amazing information from so many awesome professional star speakers that my head was about to explode. I loved every minute of that conference although I probably don't remember anything I was so overwhelmed. Buy the end of the first day, I wanted to introduce myself to every cool speaker in the room and tell them I wanted to be just like them even though I didn't know how to start, or what to do, or where to go for help.

And then I saw a tall, lanky man with a crew cut come on stage and I was transfixed. He was a classically trained guitarist who used rock and roll music in his speaking presentation on the subject "What If…" He was giving a talk on marketing in a machine gun style. He struck me as totally brilliant. I don't think I heard very much of what he said because I was only thinking how I wanted this man to be my speech coach. I wanted Mike Rayburn to coach me and get me on a fast track and launch me as a professional speaker. And that's when I knew that there was going to be a natural transition from author to speaker and a new journey was about to begin. It was then that I realized that I was developing a new passion.

After Mike Rayburn's presentation, I tried to corner him as fast as I could. I had to wait until he talked to three people who were lined up in front of me. I stood impatiently for my turn.

"I want you to be my speech coach," I blurted out to Mike as I walked up to him. Mike looked a little shocked and then he smiled at me. "Would you?" I asked with forced politeness.

"Why?" he asked quickly. "Why me?"

"Because you are a performer and so am I. You'll understand my energy and how I can channel that energy into the speaking world and I think you are the one that can put me on a fast tract," I replied with more boldness than I needed.

I had no right to ask Mike to take me on as a client. Some professional speakers don't even like to coach because they are too busy building their own careers. Yet, I had a feeling he wouldn't turn me down. He even lived in Las Vegas and was also a stage entertainer on the Las Vegas Strip from time to time. I was talking as fast as I could, telling him about my family in Las Vegas, and how I had lived in that city for eighteen years and what I did for a living. I even gave him a copy of *60, Sex & Tango, Confessions of a Beatnik Boomer*.

"If you have time, please read this. It might give you some idea if you want to take me on as a client." Then I slipped him my card.

Mike smiled and took the book. "I'll be in touch," he said kindly.

In March of that year, Mike and I met at a coffee shop somewhere in east Las Vegas. He ate breakfast while I watched him nervously. We talked small talk, then some big talk, and after he finished breakfast we came to a meeting of the minds.

"I'll take you on as a client," he finally said. "You're going to do great things. Let's get you a topic first."

Mike coached me for over a year and we produced three speeches together. We had many moments of amazing intensity, inspiration and great story telling. After that first year, he gave me legs to walk and wings to fly into the speaking profession. I gave twenty speeches in the last nine months, which qualified me for membership in the National Speakers Association. That was a goal I had hoped to accomplish. My coach was beaming when I told him.

What I am most proud of is my learning curve. Besides the fact that I now text message with everyone in my universe, I blog, twitter, check my Facebook page weekly and have actual social media tools at my disposal. And throughout the difficult and challenging year and a half, I have never lost my passion about being a professional speaker. It is a joyful path for me because of my belief in my message.

I still teach yoga and meditation at UCLA and love every class and every one of my yoga students. I continue to enjoy my family, especially watching my five grandchildren grow and learn new things. I have a close relationship with my adult sons, perhaps deeper and more meaningful than ever before. I say that, of course, with trepidation that it could change any minute. I'm keeping my fingers crossed that we hold on to what we've got.

Oh, yes, maybe, just maybe I have finally found love!

NOTES

www.ingramcontent.com/pod-product-compliance
Lightning Source LLC
Chambersburg PA
CBHW031238290426
44109CB00012B/348